ISO 9000

Other McGraw-Hill Quality Books of Interest

ISO 9000

Meeting the New International Standards

Perry L. Johnson

McGraw-Hill, Inc.

New York   San Francisco   Washington, D.C.   Auckland   Bogotá
Caracas   Lisbon   London   Madrid   Mexico City   Milan
Montreal   New Delhi   San Juan   Singapore
Sydney   Tokyo   Toronto

Library of Congress Cataloging-in-Publication Data

Johnson, Perry L. (Perry Lawrence), date.
ISO 9000 : meeting the new international standards / Perry L.
Johnson.
  p. cm.
Includes bibliographical references and index.
ISBN 0-07-032691-6 (alk. paper)
  1. Quality control—Standards. 2. Manufactures—Quality control—
Standards. I. Title.
TS156.J656 1993
658.5′62—dc20   93-7938
                           CIP

1 2 3 4 5 6 7 8 9 0 DOC/DOC 9 9 8 7 6 5 4 3

ISBN 0-07-032691-6

*The sponsoring editor for this book was Harold B. Crawford, the editing supervisor
was Stephen M. Smith, and the production supervisor was Pamela A. Pelton. It was
set in Baskerville by Carol Woolverton, Lexington, Massachusetts, in cooperation
with Warren Publishing Services, Eastport, Maine.*

Printed and bound by R. R. Donnelley & Sons Company.

This book is printed on recycled, acid-free paper containing a
minimum of 50 percent recycled de-inked fiber.

You don't have to do this.
Survival is not compulsory.

DR. W. EDWARDS DEMING,
on the importance of ISO 9000

Contents

Preface

The ISO 9000 quality system standard is much more than just the latest wave of the worldwide drive for quality, for unlike other quality programs, practices, and procedures, ISO 9000 is international in scope and impact. Moreover, ISO 9000 has practical, dollars-and-cents implications for American business, in both the short and long run.

In the short run, implementation of an ISO 9000 quality system has a major and positive impact on quality, productivity, and cost reduction. And registration to ISO 9000 can give American businesses unmatched credibility and competitive advantage in the newly emerging European Community.

In the long run, implementation of ISO 9000—and registration to the standard—will preserve and create domestic and international markets for American businesses in virtually every field. Even now, ISO 9000 is starting to appear as an option—if not a requirement—on the supplier quality assurance qualification listings for many major American businesses and government institutions.

This book was written to provide managers, engineers, and businesspeople of all disciplines—especially those not especially versed in the quality technologies—with comprehensive information about the ISO 9000 standard and its applications.

The information in this book comes from a wide range of sources. The most important of these is the official *ISO 9000: International*

Standards for Quality Management, published by the ISO in Geneva, Switzerland. Firms that are serious about ISO 9000 should rely upon these documents.

Firms planning to adopt ISO 9000 should also obtain the aid of accredited ISO 9000 consultants in interpreting the standard to their specific situation. Although much effort was put forth to make this book accurate and helpful, it should be relied upon only as a general guide.

In addition, numerous articles and other printed material about the ISO 9000 standard were consulted. A list of these sources appears in the Bibliography.

Finally, the help of a number of ISO 9000 consultants and implementors in Europe, England, and North America is appreciated. Several dozen managers of American firms that have obtained, or are in the process of obtaining, ISO 9000 registration shared their experiences and views, and many of these appear in this book. For various reasons, some asked that their comments appear unattributed. The names of the rest appear in the Acknowledgments, and thanks go out to all.

Perry L. Johnson

Acknowledgments

The following individuals contributed to the creation of this book by participating in interviews, surveys, and other research efforts. Deepest thanks are extended for their cooperation.

Bradford Aho, Magnetic Data, Inc., Eden Prairie, Minnesota

Jeff Armstrong, H. P. Smith, Iowa City, Iowa

Mark Beale, Ceco Filters, Conshohocken, Pennsylvania

Dennis Beckley, Dayton-Rogers, Minneapolis, Minnesota

David Beckwith, Powdertech Corp., Valparaiso, Indiana

Craig Billings, Lectron Products, Bellefontaine, Ohio

Donald Blair, H. P. Smith, Bedford Park, Illinois

Keith Brown, Marmon/Keystone Corporation, Butler, Pennsylvania

Brian Burke, Container Products Corp., Southfield, Michigan

Bill Busher, Leybold Inficon, East Syracuse, New York

John Cline, Olympic Steel, Minneapolis, Minnesota

Anthony Coggeshall, Adhesives Research, Inc., Glen Rock, Pennsylvania

Mike Cook, Toppan Printronics, Dallas, Texas

David Coombes, United Kingdom

Art Coté, Delphian, Northvale, New Jersey

Frederick Douglas, Defense Research Inc., Anniston, Alabama

Joseph Druecker, Indiana Products Co., South Bend, Indiana

Jim Ecklein, Augustine Medical, Eden Prairie, Minnesota

Tim Edwards, CTS Corporation, Elkhart, Indiana

Steve Ekblad, Dayton-Rogers, Minneapolis, Minnesota

Jesus Estrada, Keptel, Inc., El Paso, Texas

Charles Funk, Ingersoll-Rand Co., Davidson, North Carolina

Mark Gill, PPG Industries, Delaware, Ohio

Ray Grote, PMI Food Equipment Group, Troy, Ohio

Timmy Hale, First Chemical Corp., Pascagoula, Mississippi

Wayne Henderlong, Powdertech Corp., Valparaiso, Indiana

Tim Jestness, American Chrome & Chemicals, Corpus Christi,
  Texas

Linda Kabel, Menasha Corporation, Coloma, Michigan

Doug Karns, Brush Wellman, Inc., Portage, Ohio

John Milsovic, H. P. Smith, Bedford Park, Illinois

Larry Montalto, Alusuisse, Bellwood, Illinois

Lorcan Mooney, United Kingdom

Charles Mortimer, Monarch Stampco, New Bremen, Ohio

Dennis Payne, Woodbridge Foam Corp., Woodbridge, Ontario

Bill Pietrzyk, USA-TACOM, Warren, Michigan

D. G. Prillaman, CTS Corporation, Elkhart, Indiana

William Rahn, Ford Motor Company, Ypsilanti, Michigan

George Raub, TRW Vehicle Safety Systems Division, Washington,
  Michigan

Mike Ruetz, Blackman Uhler Chemical, Spartanburg, South
  Carolina

Mel Sand, Federal Stampings, Rochester, New York

Julian Smith, General Motors Saginaw Division, Athens, Alabama

Tom Solomon, Federal Stampings, St. Petersburg, Florida

Mike Sweeney, CTS Corporation, Elkhart, Indiana

William Taylor, Keptel, Inc., Tinton Falls, New Jersey

John Troyer, Ford Meter Box Co., Wabash, Indiana

Dave Turtletaub, Phillips Circuit Assembly, Tampa, Florida

Don Van Hook, Strahman Valves, Inc., Florham Park, New Jersey

Mike Webb, Federal Stampings, St. Petersburg, Florida

Sandy Weller, Woodbridge Foam Corp., Woodbridge, Ontario

Noel White, United Kingdom

Wayne Williams, Kenmode Tool, Algonquin, Illinois

Stephen Wityl, Virginia Panel Corp., Waynesboro, Virginia

Larry Wojnicz, Outokumpu Copper, Kenosha, Wisconsin

ISO 9000 at a Glance

Type	Name	Description
Guidelines	ISO 9000 (1987)	Guidelines for selection and use
	ISO 9000-2 (prospective)	Guidelines for application of ISO 9001, ISO 9002, and ISO 9003
	ISO 9000-3 (1991)	Guidelines for the application of ISO 9001 to the development, supply, and maintenance of software
	ISO 8402 (1986)	Quality vocabulary
Quality systems (contractual models)	ISO 9001 (1987)	Model for quality assurance in design/development, production, installation, and servicing
	ISO 9002 (1987)	Model for quality assurance in production and installation
	ISO 9003 (1987)	Model for quality assurance in final inspection and test
Quality management and quality system elements	ISO 9004 (1987)	Guidelines
	ISO 9004-2 (1991)	Part 2: Guidelines for services

Type	Name	Description
Guidelines for auditing quality systems	ISO 10011-1 (1990)	Part 1: Auditing
	ISO 10011-2 (1991)	Part 2: Qualification criteria for quality systems auditors
	ISO 10011-3 (1991)	Part 3: Management of audit programs

ISO 9000

PART 1

All About ISO 9000

1
Today's Edge, Tomorrow's Imperative

If you do business in Europe, don't overlook new quality rules that take effect there on January 1 [1993]. . . . Businesses will have to meet [ISO 9000 international standards] in order to sell inside the European Community.

We're shooting for certification to ISO 9001. But we won't stop there. Once we've got 9001, we'll go after 9002. And then we'll knock off 9003 as well. We won't stop till we hit the top!

These quotes share three traits.

One: They concern ISO 9000, the international quality system standard.

Two: Their sources are authoritative. The first appeared in a respected American business publication; the second was stated by a prominent corporate CEO.

Three: They are erroneous.

But that is how it has been with ISO 9000. Since 1989, when ISO 9000 first began to make itself felt in the American corporate consciousness, facts have been scanty and mingled with fiction. Assorted misnomers and misleading public accounts have created chaos for American businesses that operate, or intend to operate, in Europe. At Perry Johnson, Inc., we responded to client appeals by seeking the expertise of our European associates, who have lived and worked with the ISO and related quality system standards since the 1970s. In educating our clients, we aimed, in large measure, at dispelling myths about ISO 9000.

Here are just a few.

- *ISO 9000 is "a European standard."* This claim is sometimes asserted to make ISO 9000 seem alien, unintelligible, or inappropriate to American business. The facts are that ISO 9000 was derived from home-grown American quality standards that are still in use; the United States is a member of ISO; and Americans sit on the committees responsible for the standard.

- *ISO 9000 is or will become "mandatory" in order to do business in Europe.* This is true for firms which make a relative handful of products—a list that may grow in the coming years. But the doors to Europe did not slam shut on non-ISO-registered firms on January 1, 1993. ISO 9000 registration will increasingly become desired, expected, and perhaps even required in certain markets and industries. But registration will be driven by customer requirements and competitive pressures, not via official or statutory mandate.

- *ISO 9000 is "a paperwork nightmare."* Ironically, this claim is made by American managers who think nothing of creating 500-page "quality manuals" and shelves of procedure books. Documentation is central to ISO 9000 requirements, for the purposes of planning, controlling, training, and providing objective evidence of compliance. But its requirements are minimal and in no way redundant: the typical ISO 9000 quality manual is barely 50 pages long.

- *ISO 9000 is "inspection based."* This implies that ISO 9000 is a simple "sort defects out" program. Not true. ISO 9000 requires that the quality system monitor conformance to requirements. This is just one small step in the continuous improvement cycle which is at the heart of the ISO 9000 quality system.

- *ISO 9000 is "weak on statistical techniques."* On the contrary. ISO 9000 does not require specific statistical techniques. This makes sense, because ISO 9000 is meant to be generic. It does obligate management to implement statistical techniques when and as appropriate.

- *ISO 9000 "claims to guarantee quality out the door."* This is probably the most bogus myth of all. No quality system or technique guarantees quality out the door. ISO 9000 is about meeting customer requirements with a system that is appropriate, planned, controlled, documented, and fully understood by all.

The mission of this book is to replace the myths with solid facts, such as these:

- Harmonized variants of the ISO 9000 standard have been adopted by nearly 100 nations.

- Though registrations to ISO 9000 are, as a percentage, low in Europe and far lower in the United States, the trend is upward. Firms registered to ISO 9000 are perceived to offer better quality, and have a marketplace edge over nonregistered competitors.

- Many U.S. government agencies, including the Defense Department, the FAA, and the FDA, are in the process of harmonizing their quality requirements to the ISO 9000 standard.

These facts, and a broad base of international experience providing ISO 9000 training and implementation services, lie behind the convictions which are at the heart of this book:

- By the end of the 1990s, international competitive and political pressures will cause ISO 9000 to become a major, if not preeminent, worldwide quality system—the international coin of quality.

- The merits of the ISO 9000 quality system are such that even firms unaffected by competitive and/or political pressures would do well to adopt it.

Business managers across America need to understand ISO 9000—except, of course, those who do not care about survival.

What Is ISO 9000?

ISO 9000 is the offspring of the International Organization for Standardization (ISO). Based in Geneva, Switzerland, ISO is a consortium of virtually all the world's industrialized nations—from Albania to Zimbabwe. The group's mission is to develop industrial standards that facilitate international trade. The United States is represented on ISO by the American National Standards Institute (ANSI), a very familiar name in American industry.

ISO 9000 is a not a product standard, but a *quality system standard*. It applies not to products or services, but to the process which creates them. It is designed and intended to apply to virtually any product or service made by any process anywhere in the world.

To achieve this generic state, ISO 9000 refrains, to the greatest extent possible, from mandating specific methods, practices, and techniques. It emphasizes principles, goals, and objectives. All of these focus on one objective, the same objective which drives every business: *meeting customer expectations and requirements.*

A well-designed, well-implemented, and carefully managed ISO 9000 quality system provides confidence that the output of the process will meet customer expectations and requirements. It is aimed at providing that confidence to three audiences:

- The customers directly
- The customers indirectly (via third-party assessments and quality system registration)
- Company management and staff

ISO 9000 does so by requiring that every business activity affecting quality be conducted in a three-part, never-ending cycle: planning, control, and documentation.

- Activities affecting quality must be *planned* to ensure that goals, authority, and responsibility are defined and understood.
- Activities affecting quality must be *controlled* to ensure that specified requirements (at all levels) are met, problems are anticipated and averted, and corrective actions are planned and carried out.
- Activities affecting quality must be *documented* to ensure understanding of quality objectives and methods, smooth interaction

within the organization, feedback for the planning cycle, and objective evidence of quality system performance for those who require it, such as customers or third-party assessors.

ISO 9000 is not new or radical. It is good, hardheaded, common business sense in codified, verifiable, and easily adapted form. It has strong commonalities with other quality schemes, such as MIL-Q, Deming's 14 Points, total quality management, and the Malcolm Baldrige National Quality Award criteria.

The main difference is that a firm can *register* to ISO 9000.

How ISO 9000 Is Applied

As detailed in Chap. 3, there are two broad ways to apply the ISO 9000 quality system standard. One way is to implement it for *quality management purposes*—that is, to obtain its benefits for their own sake.

The other way is to obtain *certification* or, more properly, *registration* to the ISO 9000 quality system standard. Registration provides the benefits of quality system management, plus significant strategic advantages.

Some firms seek registration for competitive reasons or because they hope ISO registration will reduce the number of supplier quality assurance (SQA) audits they must undergo. Others register because theirs is a "regulated product" as defined by the product directive of the European Community (see below). But according to a study by Britain's authoritative Institute for Quality Assurance, most firms seek ISO 9000 registration because of pressure from customers.

Registration is awarded by an accredited third-party registration body after it satisfies itself, by reviewing documentation and conducting on-site assessments (audits), that the firm's quality system conforms to the ISO 9000 standard.

ISO 9000 registration is renewable, and enforced by semiannual surveillance visits by the registration body. Registration is surprisingly easy to get, for firms which already have significant quality systems in place. Registration is also relatively easy to keep. But conformance to ISO 9000 is almost impossible to *fake*. The standard focuses on performance, documentation, and objective evidence. There are no shortcuts. You must walk your talk.

As explained more fully in Chap. 3, the benefits of registration can be substantial. ISO 9000 registration affords access to markets, an enhanced quality image, and significant competitive advantages. It also has been shown to enhance business health. The Institute for Quality Assurance has found that the annual bankruptcy rate for nonregistered British firms is 7.14 percent, while the rate for registered firms is a mere 0.2 percent.

All these benefits notwithstanding, most American firms are after ISO 9000 registration because of international considerations. Let us take a look at those.

Impact of ISO 9000

ISO 9000 is international, which means, of course, "worldwide." But since the most immediate and profound impact of ISO 9000 is upon Europe, let us survey the political stage there.

- The *European Community* (EC), established in 1958, today consists of 12 member states: Belgium, Denmark, France, Germany, Greece, Ireland, Italy, Luxembourg, the Netherlands, Portugal, Spain, and the United Kingdom. The EC comprises a marketplace of some 320 million people.

- The *European Free Trade Association* (EFTA) is a separate group of six nations: Austria, Finland, Iceland, Norway, Sweden, and Switzerland.

- The *European Economic Area* (EEA) is the collective term for the EC and the EFTA. It comprises some 380 million consumers in 18 nations. Thus the EEA represents the largest single market in the world—larger than the United States and Japan combined.

Since the adoption of the Single European Act in 1987, the EC, together with the EFTA, has been making strides toward unifying member nations into a single marketplace, under the banner "Europe 1992." The effort could ultimately result in total economic unity, including removal of internal trade barriers and adoption of a single currency.

The total vision of "Europe 1992" may never come to pass, however, because of political and cultural factors which are beyond the scope of this book. Many advances are being made nevertheless. Acting in concert, the EC Council of Ministers has adopted many policies and regulations governing the conduct of trade among member nations. Most particularly, the EC has begun requiring *product certification* for certain "regulated products." Such products cannot be marketed in the EC without independent certification as to safety and other factors.

The EC has also established guidelines for *quality system registration.* To be certified, a regulated product must be made under the aegis of a quality system that has been independently assessed and certified as meeting EC-approved quality system standards. Those standards, which the EC calls EN 29000, are in fact an exact "harmonized" equivalent of ISO 9000.

In short, ISO 9000 is the recognized, accepted, and (for certain products) mandated quality system standard in Europe. Though the doors did not slam shut on nonregistered firms on January 1, 1993, the time is rapidly coming when ISO 9000 will be the rules by which the quality game is played in the world's largest marketplace.

2
From America and Back: The Origins of the ISO 9000 Standard

ISO 9000 is more than a quality system; it is a total management system. It is the only total quality system that works.
ANTHONY COGGESHALL
Adhesives Research, Inc.
Registered to ISO 9001

The ISO 9000 quality system standard is somewhat new to American businesspeople. But most U.S. quality professionals understand the concept of quality system standards. First- and second-tier suppliers to major manufacturers such as the Big 3 automakers, as well as primary Defense Department contractors, have been subject to quality systems and audits for many years.

Some of these programs have an eerie resemblance to ISO 9000.

As Jim Ecklein of Augustine Medical, a medical devices manufacturer registered to ISO 9003, notes, "The FDA has long mandated a Good Manufacturing Practices program—which is very compatible with ISO." Augustine Medical is now seeking ISO 9001 registration. George Raub, whose TRW Vehicle Safety Systems Division is working toward registration to ISO 9001 or ISO 9002 (depending on scope), notes that ISO 9000 has many similarities to General Motors' Targets for Excellence program as well as to the Q1 program of the Ford Motor Company.

These resemblances are no accident. ISO 9000 is an "international" standard, sponsored by a Swiss-based organization and the direct descendent of a British quality system. But, like many other quality-oriented techniques such as statistical process control, the ISO 9000 standard has directly traceable American ancestry. Moreover, the United States is a member nation of ISO, and Americans participated in the formulation of the ISO 9000 standard. Thus ISO 9000 can by no means be considered "foreign" by American businesspeople.

ISO itself states that its series of international standards (ISO 9000 to ISO 9004, inclusive) "embodies a rationalization of the many and various national approaches" to quality systems. Even so, there are very real differences between the application of quality systems in the United States and in Europe. These differences are crucial to understanding the role of ISO 9000 today. In this chapter, we will trace the history and development of

- Quality standards generally
- ISO 9000's distant forebears
- ISO 9000's parents
- ISO 9000's siblings and sponsors

Standards: From Product to Quality to System

No one knows who invented the first set of "standards." But their development is key to the emergence of the high-technology age as we know it. Technological advancements and the development of standards have gone hand in hand.

Centuries ago, craftspeople made products on a highly individualized basis. Operating in cottage settings, they employed unique and highly personalized design standards. Their standards for quality were likewise individualized. Typically, quality standards were driven by individual, one-on-one customer feedback (a method which remains highly pertinent today).

In medieval times, craftsworkers began to band together to form guilds and trade unions. These groups created their own standards by which expertise in the various skills was measured. At the same time, military organizations found that the quality of the equipment and materiel they used was quite literally a matter of life and death. As a result, quality standards were imposed upon suppliers. A thousand years ago, the British king appointed an officer to oversee the production of naval ships. Another official was put in charge of the quality and effectiveness of land-based weaponry and engineering.

Standardization itself became preeminent with the dawn of the Industrial Age. Eli Whitney may be most famous for his cotton gin, but the impact of that achievement pales compared with his use of standard, interchangeable parts in the making of rifles. Military applications such as these continued to drive the development and refinement of product standards and eventually quality standards as well.

By the start of this century, quality standards were being institutionalized and documented. As far back as 1912, the British government created an office to ensure the quality of British military aircraft.

American Quality Standards

Some pinpoint the dawn of America's "quality age" with the recession of 1981–1982, the increased emergence of Japan as an economic threat, and the appearance of "Quality is Job 1" as an advertising slogan of the Ford Motor Company.

Actually, documented quality standards of various kinds have been a fact of life in the American military establishment—and among defense contractors—since World War II, when the Defense Department established its MIL STD series of standards. These standards were, as we shall see, key to the development of international quality standards as we know them today. Arguably, the most significant documented military standard is MIL-Q-9858, a quality management program adopted in 1959 by the Department of Defense. Succeeded by MIL-Q-9858A in 1963, this standard is adhered to by most suppliers to the Department of Defense.

A parallel development was the creation of supplier quality standards imposed by major manufacturers such as the Big 3 automakers and first-tier suppliers to the Defense Department. These organizations, which relied heavily on subsidiary suppliers for subassemblies and components, realized that meeting quality standards imposed upon them required them to impose quality standards upon their own suppliers.

This resulted in proprietary quality standards, such as Ford Motor Company's Q1 and General Motors' Targets for Excellence (TFE). Over the past decade, the requirements of such standards have steadily tightened. They have become more demanding and more specific as to the types of quality tools, techniques, and reporting systems suppliers are expected to use. And now many majors go beyond requiring just immediate suppliers to adhere to these standards. They also require their suppliers to require *their suppliers* to adhere to them.

In this way, a patchwork quilt of quality system standards has spread across the American corporate landscape—a kind of "domino effect." The standards can differ in significant ways, even among firms in the same marketplace. Many suppliers to these firms are subject to as many as a *dozen* competing and, sometimes, contradictory quality standards. These suppliers are often under virtually constant audit by one customer or another.

Recently, the Big 3 automakers began work to bring consistency to their various standards. This move would allow their suppliers, many of whom serve all of the Big 3, to adhere to one automotive quality standard instead of three. Obviously, suppliers like this idea. To them, a single, universally recognized and accepted quality system standard is very appealing indeed.

But dominos do not fall everywhere. Customer-mandated quality standards and programs such as Q1 and TFE have not by any means reached a majority of U.S. businesses and facilities. Many American firms and facilities remain unaffected by quality system requirements.

Quality Standards Overseas

Overseas, particularly in Britain, the development of quality system standards took a somewhat different course.

AQAP, DEF/STAN, BS . . .

If imitation is the sincerest form of flattery, then MIL-Q-9858A is a flattered program indeed. In 1968, the North Atlantic Treaty Organization (NATO) adopted it as its own quality system standard, calling it AQAP-1 (Allied Quality Assurance Publication 1). The British Department of Defence, knowing a good thing when it saw one, incorporated most of AQAP's provisions two years later in its own quality system standard called DEF/STAN 05-8.

Conventional wisdom has it that U.S. quality methods and standards are 5 to 10 years ahead of British, and that the United States has much more of a laissez-faire tradition than Britain. But the British were the first to go beyond implementing official quality standards for defense alone. This early and intense interest in quality as an international policy imperative may have stemmed from the distance British quality had to travel.

In any event, in 1979 Britain took the unprecedented step of officially adopting a quality system standard for its commercial establishment. In accordance with the philosophy of Margaret Thatcher—"Quality is about making products that don't come back for customers that do"—the British Standards Institute, at the time a government agency, developed BS 5750, a quality system standard evolved from DEF/STAN, AQAP, and MIL-Q.

In addition to promulgating the standard, the British government actively supported and promoted it. The Department of Trade and Industry, equivalent to the U.S. Department of Commerce, sponsored the body which accredits quality system registrars. It also sponsored another body which accredits quality system assessors and assessor training. (More on these issues in Chap. 13.)

Even more important, the British government vigorously promoted BS 5750 throughout the private sector. It actively encouraged firms to register, and publicized BS 5750 to increase consumer awareness and acceptance of the standard.

. . . EC, ISO, and EN

In 1987, probably the most important year in the history of postwar Europe, the Single European Act was passed by the European Community. This set a course intended to lead to the development of an economically—if not politically—united Europe.

That same year saw these landmark advances in the development of quality system standards:

- The International Standards Organization (ISO) created the ISO 9000 quality system standard, drawing upon the British standard BS 5750.
- The British "harmonized" BS 5750 with ISO 9000.
- The British modified DEF/STAN 05-8 to harmonize it with ISO 9000.
- The European Community (EC) adopted a quality standard virtually identical to ISO 9000 under the designation EN 29000.

The differences between American and European application of quality system standards are clear. In the United States, quality standards have mainly been driven by individual corporations and military imperatives. In Europe, governments (and the EC, which is becoming a supragovernment) have been much more actively involved. The role of government has critical implications for U.S. firms wishing to register to ISO 9000, as we shall see in Chap. 13.

Most industrialized nations have adopted "harmonized" versions of ISO 9000. No doubt for reasons of nationalist pride, these nations have by and large given their standards their own designations, even though the standards themselves are word for word ISO 9000. For example, ISO 9000 is still referred to as BS 5750 in the United Kingdom, NS 5801 in Norway, and CSAZ 299 in Canada (see Table 2-1).

Table 2-1. Harmonized Versions of ISO 9000

Nation	Standard
Australia	AS 3900
Belgium	NBNX50
Canada	CSAZ 299
Denmark	DS/EN 29000
France	NFX50
Germany	DIN ISO 9000
Hungary	MI 18990
India	IS 10201
Ireland	IS 300
Netherlands	NEN ISO 9000
New Zealand	NZS 5600
Norway	NS 5801
South Africa	SABS 0157
Spain	UNE 66900
Sweden	SS ISO 9000
United Kingdom	BS 5750

There is also an American version of ISO 9000. But here the standard's sponsorship and application are quite different.

ISO 9000 in America

As noted, quality in the United States has traditionally been a private-sector process driven by the customer/supplier relationship. Compared with European governments, the U.S. government has had only sparse involvement in quality. It sponsors the Malcolm Baldrige National Quality Award. It promotes the concept of total quality management through the tiny Federal Quality Institute. But the U.S. government does not mandate quality systems, sponsor training and accreditation organizations, or use its bully pulpit to promote quality awareness to the public.

ISO 9000's American variant developed without U.S. government provenance. The American Society for Quality Control (ASQC), a private industry trade group, publishes a harmonized variant of the ISO 9000 standard under the name Q90. ASQC sponsors Q90 jointly with the American National Standards Institute (ANSI), which represents the United States on ISO.

ASQC and Q90 have, at this writing, neither official U.S. sponsorship nor recognition in the EC. American facilities need to keep this vital point in mind as they make strategic decisions about ISO 9000.

ISO 9000: Common Ground or Battleground?

Are American quality standards stricter than European? Is U.S quality better too? In many respects, the answer to both questions is yes.

But ISO 9000 is by no means a "foreign" standard; its American parentage is clear. The real issue is leadership. The EC and ISO have done something the United States has not. By adopting ISO 9000 and EN 29000, raising their visibility, publicizing them, and mandating their use in critical industries, the EC has made quality a matter of national and international policy.

Moreover, the EC has created a comprehensive, yet relatively simple, straightforward, and most of all generic quality system standard. U.S. quality systems are, on the other hand, by no means universal. They affect some industries heavily—sometimes with almost ruinous redundancy—and leave others untouched. American quality standards tend to stress manufacturing and quite often mandate specific tools and techniques. And, with rare exceptions such as Ford's "Quality Is Job 1" campaign, U.S. quality programs and standards are almost unknown to the general public.

As we will see, ISO 9000 is general enough to apply to virtually any product, service, or facility, yet specific enough to create genuine and continuous improvement. It is oriented toward results rather than technique. It affects every process, every employee, and every function in the firm.

In Europe in general and Britain in particular, ISO 9000 and its equivalents enjoy strikingly high public awareness and acceptance. These are the attributes which give the ISO standard its power, and make it a force with which U.S. firms must reckon as they strive to maintain and build business in the EC.

Some have deemed ISO 9000 an attempt by the EC to erect trade barriers. But ultimately it seems futile and self-defeating to treat ISO 9000 as a battleground. ISO 9000 is in fact an *opportunity* for American businesses—an opportunity to obtain benefits: most practical, some measurable.

We turn to those benefits in the following chapter.

3
Benefits of ISO 9000

What is this, another "program of the month"?

Oh, goody. More audits.

What can these Europeans teach us about quality that we don't already know?

Americans react to ISO 9000 in various ways. In large part, they are skeptical. The main concern of any firm is a very logical one: "What's in it for me?"

For many firms, the answer is obvious. They know for a fact that, without ISO 9000, they will lose business. If your firm is in this position, the threat may manifest itself in various ways:

- The EC makes ISO 9000 registration mandatory for firms in your marketplace.
- Your biggest customer requires ISO 9000 of all suppliers.
- Your major competitor has adopted ISO 9000.

Protecting existing markets is just one of the many practical, measurable benefits that has drawn American firms in droves into the realm of ISO 9000. Other benefits are less measurable, more philosophical, and definitely of long-term orientation. They lack the dramatic immediacy of hammering the competition or saving the firm from oblivion. But they are just as profound as the more immediate kind.

The ISO 9000 quality system standard has implications both short and long term, applications both tactical and strategic. As the standard itself says, in the opening "Guidelines for Selection and Use," its objectives affect competitiveness as well as quality:

> In both these situations, the supplier's organization wants to install and maintain a quality system that will strengthen its own competitiveness and achieve the needed product quality in a cost-effective way.

In this chapter, we shall answer the question "What's in it for me?" by examining the benefits of ISO 9000. To a great extent, the range and intensity of the benefits are determined by the way the standard is applied. The structure of ISO 9000 itself acknowledges this. It provides for two broad avenues of application:

- *Quality management purposes,* in which the facility adopts the standard as a blueprint for its internal quality system

- *Contractual purposes,* in which a demonstrated quality system is a condition of a contract with a customer

The benefits obtained through contractual application of ISO 9000 include the practical, immediate advantages cited above, as well as the general, long-term benefits obtained through the development and operation of a genuine quality management system. Let us look at the quality management benefits first.

What Is a Quality System?

The aim of a quality system is to ensure that the facility's product or service (generically referred to as *output*) meets the customer's quality requirements. The quality system incorporates both quality assurance and quality control.

Fine. But what is quality? What, for that matter, are quality assurance and quality control?

The ISO 9000 standard is carefully designed. Each element is meticulously defined. Each section of the standard offers thorough definitions of the terms used, and the definitions are also gathered and presented in a document called ISO 8402, "International Standard Quality Vocabulary." Let us look at how the standard defines these critical terms.

Quality, as ISO 9000 interprets it, is an integration of the features and characteristics which determine the extent to which output satisfies the *customer*'s needs. Notice how customer-driven this definition is. Customers determine what features and characteristics are important. Customers judge the extent to which the features and characteristics of the output satisfy their needs.

Quality assurance is the collective term for planned, formalized activities intended to provide confidence that the output will meet required quality levels. In addition to in-process activities, quality assurance includes an array of activities external to the process—including, of course, activities undertaken to determine customer needs.

Quality control is the collective term for in-process activities and techniques intended to create specific quality characteristics. These activities include monitoring, reduction of variation, elimination of known causes, and efforts to increase economic effectiveness.

A quality system, then, is a management-driven, facilitywide, and processwide program of plans, activities, resources, and events. This program is implemented and managed with the aim of ensuring that process output will (1) meet customer quality requirements, logically ensuring that (2) return-on-investment (ROI) goals are met.

An effective quality system is the philosophical and procedural "glue" which unites all elements of the facility—including employees, plant, equipment, and procedures—with *suppliers* at the input end and *customers* at the output end.

Facilities which operate quality systems tend to exhibit the following attributes:

- A philosophy of prevention rather than detection
- Continuous review of critical process points, corrective actions, and outcomes

- Consistent communication within the process, and among facility, suppliers, and customers
- Thorough recordkeeping and efficient control of critical documents
- Total quality awareness by all employees
- High level of management confidence

These attributes inevitably lead to the following tangible benefits:

Informed, competent management decision making

Dependable process input (supplier control)

Control of quality costs

Increased productivity

Reduced waste

In sum, the facility with a well-designed and well-implemented quality system has a process which tends to be lean, sensitive to customer needs, highly reactive, efficient, and positioned at the leading edge of its marketplace.

These are the benefits obtainable by facilities which implement ISO 9000 for quality management purposes. Implementation is achieved by following the guidelines in ISO 9004 (for manufacturing) and/or ISO 9004-2 (for service). These "parts," or components, of the ISO 9000 standard are defined in Chap. 4.

Most often, facilities get involved with the ISO 9000 quality system standard for *contractual* purposes—that is, because a customer has specified an ISO 9000 quality system as a condition of the contract. Such a condition usually requires the facility to become *registered* to the standard.

ISO 9000 Registration

Facilities which register to ISO 9000 obtain all the benefits of quality management users—plus a few more. Before detailing these, let us take a brief look at the ISO 9000 registration process. (The process is examined in detail in Chap. 13.)

A facility seeks *registration* to ISO 9000 for one or more of the following reasons:

1. One or more customers require it by contract.
2. The facility expects such contractual requirements to be imposed at some point.
3. The facility views the registration approach as the most logical and effective way to implement and manage the quality system.

Unlike "quality management" applications of ISO 9000, which do not involve firms outside the facility, registration requires involvement with outside agents, called *registrars*. Registrars are specially accredited for this purpose, and the process of selecting the correct one for your needs can be tricky. (The selection process is detailed in Chap. 13.)

ISO 9000 certification may be awarded on a per-facility, rather than per-firm, basis. Therefore, a firm with 10 facilities may need to acquire 10 certifications. Certification is conferred when the registrar satisfies itself, by means of audits of the process and its documentation, that the facility

- Has a quality system which meets the ISO 9000 standard
- Uses that system actively in its daily course of activities

The facility becomes certified to one of three "parts" of the ISO 9000 standard. These parts, called ISO 9001, 9002, and 9003, are actually quality system models. The facility becomes certified to the model which most closely fits the scope of its operations, as described in detail in the next chapter.

The facility's quality system need include only those elements of the standard which are relevant to the effective operation of the facility. The system must be documented through one or more levels of documentation, including, for most facilities, a "quality manual" as the top tier.

Certification, once awarded, is reinforced—and enforced—by means of semiannual on-site audits. These "surveillance visits" review any changes to the quality system and ensure that corrective actions called for under previous assessments have been carried out.

Benefits of Registration

One benefit of registration is that the facility regularly undergoes objective assessment by outside quality professionals. That alone is a powerful argument for registration. There are three other compelling reasons as well: access to markets, competitive issues, and potential net reduction in audits.

Access to Markets.   Access to markets is the most critical benefit of ISO 9000 certification. It enables facilities to maintain or create customer relationships in situations in which ISO 9000 certification is required.

As noted in Chap. 1, the EC Council of Ministers now mandates ISO 9000 certification for makers of certain types of products. These include commercial scales, construction products, gas appliances, industrial safety equipment, medical devices, and telecommunications terminal equipment. More products may be added to this list via additional product directives. This is especially likely for products and services that are potentially hazardous, that involve personal safety, or that are otherwise affected by product liability or similar regulations.

But at this time such "mandated" ISO 9000 registrations are rare. Today, the pressure for ISO registration is almost purely driven by nongovernment forces. Some major firms in Europe and elsewhere are moving toward mandating ISO 9000 registration by their suppliers.

Dennis Beckley of Dayton-Rogers has found this to be the case. His facility is working toward ISO 9002 registration. "One customer said to us, 'I'm being forced to find ISO 9000 registered vendors. Once I find one, it's going to get all my business.'"

Woodbridge Foam Corp., a candidate for ISO 9002 registration, has experienced similar pressure. "One of our biggest customers," says Sandy Weller, "asked about ISO a while back. Now they're requiring it. They're giving us a year to get registered."

And Anthony Coggeshall of Adhesives Research, which has a major commercial presence in the EC, saw ISO pressure coming long ago: "Our customers started asking for it as far back as late 1990, early 1991." Adhesives Research has registered to ISO 9001.

For firms like these, the "benefit" of certification is that it enables them to retain their existing markets.

Competitive Issues. Other firms are moving toward ISO 9000 registration because of *competitive threats.*

Take Menasha Corporation. "One of our competitors," says Linda Kabel, "let it be known that they will be certified by end of next year. So now our customer wants to know if we are going to be certified, too." Ironically, Kabel was already in the process of implementing an ISO 9001 quality system. "We were using it as a guideline to setting up a whole quality process," she says. "But now there's all kinds of urgency. Our sales manager is putting on major pressure, saying we could lose our customer if we don't get certified."

At this time, most of the pressure is not in the nature of requirements or competitive threats. Rather, it is commercial pressure arising simply from stiffening international competition and the needs of firms everywhere to differentiate among their suppliers.

George Raub of TRW asserts: "One of our major overseas accounts is asking very pointed questions about our plans for ISO 9000."

Don Van Hook of Strahman Valves, an ISO 9001 candidate, describes the inquiries of one of the firm's European distributors: "They're selling in the EC, and they're thinking they'll have to require certification sometime. We know they're very sensitive to the issue of ISO certification. So we're moving on it."

Monarch Stampco is seeking ISO 9002 registration simply because the ISO 9000 standard is receiving greater and greater attention. "I'm seeing ISO 9000 mentioned more and more on RFQs," says Charles Mortimer.

Perhaps your facility does not fall into the categories above. If that is the case, then the major benefit of certification may be the clear *competitive edge* it will give you over facilities which are not certified.

Certified facilities are authorized to display a special mark, or logo. EC firms understand and value the significance of that mark. As quality becomes an increasingly vital differentiator in the marketplace, ISO-certified facilities will enjoy a clear competitive advantage.

Potential Audit Reduction. The final benefit of ISO 9000 registration—and for the most part merely a speculative one at this point—is the potential for reduced audits. Many facilities in certain industry segments undergo dozens of customer quality audits each year—some as many as 30 per month! As ISO 9000 registration becomes understood and accepted in the United States, it is possible and perhaps even likely that many customers will accept current ISO 9000 registration in lieu of site audits, mail-in audits, or other redundant "supplier quality assurance" programs.

That is certainly the hope of Brian Burke of Container Products: "We believe that once our quality system is ISO certified, we'll be exempted from some of our larger customers' supplier audits."

ISO 9000 registration, then, gives the facility the benefit of an objectively evaluated and enforced quality system. It offers the potential of reducing time-consuming and expensive supplier audits in the future. And it offers a powerful strategic benefit for facilities having current or planned business ties with the EC, including:

- Facilities located in the EC, actively making and/or marketing products or services there

- Facilities with corporate ties to firms making and/or marketing products or services in the EC

- Facilities which export to the EC

The Bottom Line

ISO 9000 is an ideal quality system for facilities which are serious about quality. It is an emerging imperative for any facility which has, or expects to have, commerce with EC nations. And certification provides the EC-hungry facility with an incomparable competitive edge.

These, along with the quality system benefits cited above, make achievement of ISO 9000 standards a powerful strategic tool, whether the facility goes the certification route or not. Many firms, such as Augustine Medical, have already benefited from registration. As Jim Ecklein notes: "It's opened a lot of doors for us; our European theater has taken off like gangbusters." Anthony Coggeshall of Adhesives Research concurs: "It's opened doors to sales that were closed to us before, especially some of the medical markets to whom we were simply an unknown. That changed once they saw that we were ISO registered."

Voices of the Users: What ISO 9000 Achieves

We expect to see significant productivity improvements.
Art Coté, Delphian, Northvale, NJ

[We expect ISO to give us] a competitive edge.
Wayne Williams, Kenmode Tool, Algonquin, IL

We're looking for better control and to retain customers who require ISO 9000. *Mike Sweeney, WTS Corporation, Elkhart, IN*

[ISO 9000] improves productivity, reduces costs, reduces process scrap. We expect to earn additional world market share.
John Troyer, Ford Meter Box Co., Wabash, IN

We hope ISO 9000 will help us get easier certification by customers. *William H. Taylor III, Keptel Inc., Tinton Falls, NJ*

We're seeking ISO 9000 registration in order to continue business in Europe.
Stephen F. Wityl, Virginia Panel Corp., Waynesboro, VA

We are pursuing certification because we expect a higher level of access and credibility with our customers, current and potential, who market in Europe.
Mike Ruetz, Blackman Uhler Chemical, Spartanburg, SC

The testimony of satisfied users continues. And with it, the list of potential benefits of ISO 9000 registration grows.

4

Components of the ISO 9000 Standard

Let's face it: Nobody likes quality. Quality in America bears the stigma of being the industrial cop. For all the preaching about quality, it is still seen as a necessary evil by American manufacturing. But ISO 9000 is different. ANTHONY COGGESHALL
Adhesives Research Inc.
Registered to ISO 9001

More than anything, ISO 9000 is a method of managing the quality process. It requires a real change in your corporate paradigm and attitude in looking at quality. BRIAN BURKE
Container Products Co.
ISO 9002 Candidate

ISO 9000 has become a sweeping generic term, a topic, a subject heading. As the offspring of many parents, it has been reviewed, revised, amended, and emended by many over the years. This constant overhauling has made ISO 9000 almost, but not quite, a "horse designed by committee." It has also made the standard and its compo-

31

nents less than user friendly and has led to a certain level of confusion among those seeking information on the subject.

Moreover, since the current ISO 9000 boom began in 1991, the topic has been written about and discussed by many people and publications all over the world. Unfortunately, the volume of editing, revision, and discussion, and in some cases poorly informed opinion, has led to a certain amount of imprecision and error with respect to the standard. To illustrate the point, two more myths can be dispelled:

- ISO 9000 does have a precise meaning beyond its usage as a generic term or subject heading. It is the official designation of the overseeing document that describes the quality system standard (see below).

- ISO 9000 registration is a bit of a misnomer. A facility does not become registered to ISO 9000; it becomes registered to one of the three contractual quality system models: ISO 9001, 9002, or 9003.

To remove confusion, let us go straight to the source: the array of documents embodying the ISO 9000 standard. The parent documents are published and distributed by ISO. Harmonized variants are also published under the various national schemes listed in Chap. 3. These documents describe the elements of the quality system standard in detail, including:

Quality system requirements

Quality system recommendations

Guidelines for selection and use

The documents also provide supporting information, such as definitions of terms, guidelines for assessors and assessments, standards for measuring equipment, and rules applying to the accreditation of registrars.

This chapter examines the structure of the ISO 9000 quality system standard as it is presented by the documents which embody it.

Quality System Models

Three documents—ISO 9001, 9002, and 9003—are the heart of the quality system standard as it is commonly applied today. They apply to facilities which seek ISO 9000 registration for "contractual" purposes—that is, because customers have made adherence to an ISO 9000 quality system a condition of doing business.

Sometimes the contract specifies the model to which the facility must adhere. In such a case, the facility has no trouble deciding which model to conform to. At other times, no specific contractual requirements are in place, but the facility anticipates a contractual obligation. In such a case, the facility first selects the model which most closely fits the scope of its operation. The facility then:

- Implements a quality system which conforms to the requirements of the model

- Obtains registration—independent and verifiable evidence that the facility's quality system is consistent with and meets the requirements of that model

The contents of the contractual models are described in detail near the end of this chapter. Implementation of ISO 9000 quality systems and registration to the standard are covered later in the book.

Quality Management Guidelines

ISO 9000 is not just for the facility which is, or expects to be, under contractual obligation. The standard also provides guidance for the facility wishing to implement an ISO 9000 quality system for its inherent benefits. Such facilities utilize ISO 9000's *quality management guidelines.*

These documents—ISO 9004, 9004-2, and 9000-3—are in fact quality system models. But facilities do not register to these guidelines. Quality systems based thereon are not subject to assessment. The guidelines simply spell out comprehensive quality management systems adaptable by virtually any organization.

The quality management guidelines serve another important purpose. ISO 9004 and 9004-2 can, and should, be consulted by facilities developing quality systems based upon the contractual models. Many of the passages in the guidelines serve to elucidate and expand upon the relatively pithy provisions of the contractual models. The guidelines themselves are not inherently enforceable as a condition of registration to any of the contractual models.

Guidelines for Auditing

An essential element of an ISO 9000 quality system is the continuous gathering and evaluation of objective evidence about the performance of the system against specified requirements. One way this evidence is obtained is through audits, or assessments. There are three kinds of assessments:

- *Internal assessments,* carried out by facility personnel in accordance with the facility's quality policy. Internal assessments are a requirement of the contractual models.

- *Second-party assessments,* wherein a customer audits the facility's quality system. These assessments were a common part of the American quality scene even before the advent of ISO 9000.

- *Third-party assessments,* or extrinsic audits. These audits are usually carried out by an accredited third party, often a registration body, to provide objective evidence (followed by a seal of approval) that the facility's quality system meets the published standards. In the context of this discussion, audit approval results in *registration* to the ISO 9000 quality system standard.

ISO publishes three documents governing the conduct of audits. These documents comprise the so-called ISO 10011 series, titled "Guidelines for Auditing Quality Systems."

- *ISO 10011-1 (1990),* "Auditing," establishes basic audit principles, criteria, and practices. It spells out a system governing all aspects of quality system audits, from audit planning through following up on corrective action requests.

- *ISO 10011-2 (1990),* "Qualification Criteria for Quality Systems Auditors," outlines educational, training, personal, and experiential requirements for quality system auditors and lead auditors.

- *ISO 10011-3 (1990),* "Management of Audit Programs," provides important guidelines for organizing, staffing, and carrying out audits. While general enough to apply to all types of audits, its principles should be observed as facilities develop internal audit programs consistent with the ISO 9000 standard.

Guidelines for Measuring Equipment

A facility utilizing an ISO 9000 quality system monitors critical quality characteristics on a planned basis to assess conformance to requirements. The standard does not specify how to do so. It is up to facility management to determine what is appropriate and to plan and conduct the operations accordingly.

For many facilities, however, monitoring means taking measurements. The process requires the selection, confirmation, and periodic audit of measuring equipment. The effectiveness of measurements, and decisions taken as a result, is so critical that ISO publishes a standard called "quality assurance requirements for measuring equipment."

This detailed guidance document, known as ISO 10012-1 (1992), can be agreed to as needed between individual facilities and their customers. It spells out the following requirements covering measuring equipment:

Selection

Confirmation

Audit and review

Measurement uncertainty

Confirmation procedures

Recordkeeping

Handling nonconformances

Storage and handling

Traceability

Personnel issues

The document also includes implementation guidance, definitions, and a reference section.

Supporting Documents

A number of other documents provide insight, support, interpretation, and guidance to the principal ISO 9000 quality system documents mentioned above. Here are a few.

- *ISO 9000*, subtitled "Quality Management and Quality Assurance Standards: Guidelines for Selection and Use," provides a brief introduction to the standard. It includes definitions and guidelines on how to apply the standard for quality management and contractual purposes.

- *ISO 8402*, a "quality vocabulary," is a glossary of terms used in the various documents that describe the standard.

- *ISO 9000-2*, which as of this writing has not been officially approved by ISO, contains very valuable generic guidelines for the application of the contractual models ISO 9001, 9002, and 9003.

ISO 9000 for Quality Management Purposes: The Guidance Documents

ISO 9004, 9004-2, and 9000-3 are the parts of the standard used by facilities which wish to implement quality systems but have no contractual obligation to do so. That said, it should also be stressed that facilities seeking registration to ISO 9001, 9002, or 9003 would be wise to consult these guidance documents as well.

Arguably, ISO 9004 and ISO 9004-2 provide a clearer and more graphic illustration of an integrated quality system than do the contractual models. ISO 9000-3 is a specialized set of guidelines for applying ISO 9001 to facilities which develop and maintain computer software.

All three documents provide amplification, clarification, and additional guidance on the topics covered in the contractual models. In addition, they address certain issues which are not covered in the contractual models but which are important to the effective operation of quality systems. Examples are quality costs and product safety and liability.

ISO 9004 can (and should) be consulted by both manufacturing and service-oriented facilities. ISO 9004-2 is written specifically for organizations in the service sector. But most manufacturing firms have at least some service element within their scope of operations, so it is wise for managers to be familiar with both sets of guidelines.

Both ISO 9004 and ISO 9004-2 are constructed around a graphic device called a *quality loop*. We will look closely at that loop in Chap. 5. For now, it is sufficient to say that the quality loop illustrates the major components of the quality system in circular form, basically beginning and ending with customers. Both documents go on to provide guidelines for the development and application of quality systems (see Table 4-1).

In Part 2 of this book we examine the specific technical requirements and guidelines of the ISO 9000 standard, including the recommendations in ISO 9004 and ISO 9004-2. Keep in mind that these documents contain no requirements per se, only recommendations.

ISO 9000 for Contractual Purposes: The Quality System Models

The contractual quality system models—ISO 9001, 9002, and 9003—contain the ISO 9000 "requirements" for facilities seeking to become registered to the standard (see Table 4-2). Facilities become registered to the "part" of the standard which is required by the contract and/or which most closely reflects the scope of the facility's process.

ISO 9001 is the most comprehensive part of the standard. It covers facilities whose process includes design or development, production, installation, and servicing. It contains 20 sections describing various elements of the quality system.

The scope of ISO 9002 is more limited. It applies to facilities making products which are designed and serviced by others. ISO 9002 includes 18 of the 20 sections found in ISO 9001; the wording of these sections is virtually identical.

ISO 9003 is the most limited part of the standard. It applies only to facilities performing final inspection and test functions. It includes 12 of the 20 sections found in ISO 9001. Again, the wording of these sections is virtually identical to that in ISO 9001 and ISO 9002.

Aside from the differences among the parts, these models are

Table 4-1. ISO 9004 Cross-Reference

Section	ISO 9004	Section	ISO 9004-2
0	Introduction		
1	Scope and field of application	1	Scope
2	References	2	Normative references
3	Definitions	3	Definitions
4	Management responsibility	4	Characteristics of services
5	Quality system principles	5	Quality system principles
6	Economics—quality-related cost considerations	6	Quality system operational elements
7	Quality in marketing		
8	Quality in specification and design		
9	Quality in procurement		
10	Quality in production		
11	Control of production		
12	Product verification		
13	Control of measuring and test equipment		
14	Nonconformity		
15	Corrective action		
16	Handling and post-production functions		
17	Quality documentation and records		
18	Personnel		
19	Product safety and liability		
20	Use of statistical methods		

Table 4-2. ISO 9001–9003 Cross-Reference

Section coverage	Section number		
	ISO 9001	ISO 9002	ISO 9003
Management responsibility	4.1	4.1	4.1
Quality system	4.2	4.2	4.2
Contract review	4.3	4.3	—
Design control	4.4	—	—
Document control	4.5	4.4	4.3
Purchasing	4.6	4.5	—
Purchaser-supplied product	4.7	4.6	—
Product identification and traceability	4.8	4.7	4.4
Process control	4.9	4.8	—
Inspection and testing	4.10	4.9	4.5
Inspection, measuring, and test equipment	4.11	4.10	4.6
Inspection and test status	4.12	4.11	4.7
Control of nonconforming product	4.13	4.12	4.8
Corrective action	4.14	4.13	—
Handling, storage, packaging, and delivery	4.15	4.14	4.9
Quality records	4.16	4.15	4.10
Internal quality audits	4.17	4.16	—
Training	4.18	4.17	4.11
Servicing	4.19	—	—
Statistical techniques	4.20	4.18	4.12

meant to be generic. They apply to virtually any facility producing any product or service for virtually any market. ISO has, in fact, stated that it will issue no industry-specific or interpretive quality system guidelines. That task is left to specific industries to carry out if they wish. Keeping the ISO standard as generic as possible maximizes ease of translation and applicability throughout the industrialized world.

As you examine the requirements and guidelines of ISO 9000, you will find nothing radical or new. The standard is, in fact, a common-sense mix of sound business practices and time-proven quality methods. The focus is not on products or services; it is on the facility's quality system—the network of activities designed and operated to ensure that output meets the ultimate business objective: satisfying the customer.

The ISO 9000 standard stresses objectives, not methods; concepts, not procedures. For example, the standard does not require inspection, only that output be verified in accordance with documented procedures. The standard does not mandate statistical techniques, only that management implement techniques appropriate to the facility's system. Finally, the standard gives no criteria whatever for product or service features: hardness, durability, response time, and the like.

Instead, the requirements and guidelines of the ISO 9000 standard are an intentionally bare-bones blueprint of the ideal quality system. Next, in Part 2, we shall take a detailed look at that blueprint.

PART 2

Technical Requirements and Guidelines

As discussed in Chap. 4, the heart of ISO 9000 is a series of models and several sets of guidelines. Each applies to facilities engaged in a specific scope of activities, utilizing ISO 9000 for a specific purpose.

- Facilities wishing to register to ISO 9000 adhere to one of the contractual models—ISO 9001, 9002, or 9003, depending upon their scope of operation.
- Manufacturing facilities which do not seek registration but wish to implement a quality system consistent with the standard rely upon ISO 9004 (1987) for guidance.
- Service facilities which do not seek certification but wish to implement a quality system consistent with the standard rely upon ISO 9004-2 (1991).

There are, then, three quality system models for registration purposes, and two guidance documents for facilities wishing to adhere to ISO 9000 for quality management purposes. ISO 9001, 9002, and 9003 contain the "requirements"—although not everything in those models is in fact required; some passages include qualifiers such as "where appropriate." ISO 9004 and ISO 9004-2 are guidelines, not requirements per se. They can, and should, be consulted for guidance by facilities seeking certification to the contractual models.

If this is not confusing enough, the 20 sections of ISO 9001, 18 sections of 9002, and 12 sections of 9003 are not consistently numbered. And their sections, while covering much the same subject matter as the "guidance" documents 9004 and 9004-2, are in completely different order.

In developing an ISO 9000 quality system, many facilities find it necessary to draw upon more than one of the models or guidelines. This is because many facilities are engaged in both manufacture and service in varying proportions. A maker of automotive subassemblies, for example, is almost purely involved in manufacture and only slightly involved in service. Restaurants are a virtual 50-50 mix between the two. Law offices are facilities providing 90 percent service and only 10 percent—or less—product.

In order to design an appropriate ISO 9000 quality system, managers should become familiar with all technical requirements and recommendations, whether for manufacturing or for service. The full array of technical requirements and recommendations is explored in the following chapters.

For coherence, and to eliminate the repetition, confusion, and redundancy inherent among the various documents, the various requirements have been organized and reordered by subject. Appendix A provides a detailed cross-reference, by subject and section number(s), among the various models and guidelines.

Because the standard itself is worded fairly generally, the presentation of the requirements is general, too. The applicability of any particular passage depends on the nature and scope of the facility in question. Many requirements apply to all facilities; others apply to varying degrees; still others do not apply to certain facilities at all. For example, facilities seeking registration to ISO 9002 will have no use for the design or service sections.

The following chapters are intended to provide a reliable guide to the technical requirements and recommendations of ISO

9000, and the principles behind them. It is up to facility managers to apply these requirements to their own facility and process in order to determine exactly what their particular ISO 9000 quality system needs. Appendix B presents a self-assessment checklist to aid facility managers in this process. For definitive help, the guidance of an experienced ISO 9000 counselor or registrar is strongly recommended.

One last word: Not *every* reader has the need or desire to become immersed in the minutiae of the standard. So each section begins with a brief summary in checklist form of *requirements* and *recommendations* of the section under discussion. The text which follows each summary provides details, explanations, and comments for readers who want more in-depth coverage of the material.

Finally, all readers are encouraged to read the standards themselves.

Glossary of Terms

Customer
: The recipient of a supplier's output; may be internal as well as external.

Facility
: A product or service provider which is adopting an ISO 9000 quality system. (Same as *supplier.*)

Output
: Shorthand for "products or services."

Subcontractor
: An entity providing output for the use of a supplier or facility.

Supplier
: A product or service provider which is adopting an ISO 9000 quality system. (Same as *facility.*)

5

Developing and Managing the Quality System

What I expect to have with ISO 9001 is a finely tuned quality system which gives us a smooth flow of information throughout the product cycle, from cradle to grave.

JIM ECKLEIN
*Augustine Medical
Registered to ISO 9003
ISO 9001 Candidate*

ISO 8402, the quality management vocabulary, defines a quality system as "the organizational structure, responsibilities, procedures, processes, and resources needed to implement quality management." Every section of the standard concerns the quality system, of course. But several sections specify and define the basic components:

Management Responsibility

Quality System

Quality Costs

Internal Quality Audits

Personnel and Training

These requirements are integral to the quality system and affect virtually every kind of facility which adheres to the standard. They are examined in detail below.

Management Responsibility: ISO 9001, 4.1; ISO 9004-2, 5.2

Checklist of Requirements

- Management designates a representative with authority and responsibility for implementing and maintaining the requirements of the standard.
- Management establishes, documents, and publicizes its policy, objectives, and commitment to quality and customer satisfaction.
- Management defines the responsibility, authority, and relationships for all employees whose work affects quality.
- Management conducts in-house verification and review of the quality system.

Every quality guru from Deming on has asserted that the success of a quality system is directly related to the consistency and intensity of top management's commitment. The requirements and guidelines of ISO 9000 acknowledge the truth of this assertion. The Management Responsibility requirements, which come first in the standard, place the burden directly on top management, where it belongs. The ISO 9000 guidelines document states this bluntly: "The responsibility for quality management belongs to top management."

In sum, the standard obligates management to define its quality policy and execute it through an organization of people and resources. Management is also obliged to participate actively in the quality system by conducting verification and review activities.

First of all, the standard requires top management to designate a *management representative* (MR). This individual bears day-to-day responsibility for the quality system and for adherence to the standard. The MR should possess sufficient rank and authority within the facility to be able to develop, monitor, and change elements of the quality system. The MR's other responsibilities usually include liaison with the registrar and oversight of the facility's internal audit program.

The standard also requires management—at the *highest* levels—to create and document a quality policy. The policy should address the following issues: acceptable quality levels, the facility's quality image and reputation, quality objectives, strategy for achieving those objectives, and responsibility of employees for executing the strategy.

ISO tacitly recognizes that in many firms quality policies are formulated—often after much roaring and screaming—and then promptly filed away and forgotten. The standard does not permit this to happen (at least the "filed and forgotten" part). It requires that the quality policy be documented and publicized regularly so that it is "understood" at all levels of the facility. The facility must be able to show how awareness is achieved on an ongoing basis with new and existing employees.

Under the Management Responsibility section, top management is also required to define responsibility, authority, and relationships for all employees whose work affects quality. This does not necessarily result in lengthy, formal job descriptions. Job descriptions are one option; work instructions are another. The objective set by this section is eminently reasonable to any responsible manager: to organize the facility in such a way that the work is carried out by people who understand what to do, how to do it, and how to deal with one another. As with so many other requirements of the standard, this one specifies the end, not the means.

The standard further acknowledges that change is a constant and that quality systems are never perfect. Management must pay consistent attention to the quality system to make sure that it improves and adjusts to change. Accordingly, the standard calls upon management to conduct regular *verification* of the quality system and the processes which it governs. Verification activities must be carried out only by people who do not have direct responsibility for the activities being verified. One form of verification is the *internal audit,* which we shall examine later in this chapter.

In addition, the MR and other members of management are responsible for conducting regular, documented *management reviews* of the quality system. These reviews consider, at a minimum:

- The results of internal quality audits
- Management effectiveness
- Defects and irregularities
- Resolution of customer complaints
- Solutions to quality problems
- Implementation of past solutions
- Handling of nonconforming product
- Results of statistical scorekeeping tools
- Impact of quality methods on actual results

Reviews must be conducted at "appropriate intervals" and must, of course, be fully documented. Management must show that it uses the results of these reviews as a basis for improving the quality system in particular and the facility's quality in general.

As befits the section which comes first, Management Responsibility is arguably the most important component of the standard. Its placement confirms what quality professionals have always known: that management responsibility is an absolute prerequisite to the successful pursuit of quality.

Quality System: ISO 9001, 4.2; ISO 9004-2, 5.3.3, 5.4.1-2

Checklist of Requirements

- System for developing and implementing quality plans should be considered for new products, services, or processes.
- System should provide adequate and continuous control over all activities directly affecting quality.
- Responsibility, authority, and lines of communication among all activities contributing to quality must be clearly defined.
- System should ensure that facility staff fully understand the quality system as it pertains to their areas of responsibility.

- System should provide for adequate resources to enable quality objectives to be met, with due consideration given to required levels of experience, training, and general competence levels of personnel.

- Methods for identifying, resolving, and preventing potential quality problems should be established.

- Process for reviewing and improving the quality system should be quantified.

- Methods for identification, distribution, collection, maintenance, and revisions of all quality documents and records must be established.

- Methods for collecting and retaining objective evidence resulting from day-to-day operation of the quality system must be defined.

Most facilities have quality systems of one form or another. Some are intricate and extensive. Others are rudimentary. Though "quality systems" are what ISO 9000 is all about, the standard does not oblige facilities to "add on" a separate and sometimes redundant structure. Instead, the standard:

- Describes the *ideal* quality system in illustrative form

- Sets forth *commonsense goals* for an adequate or acceptable quality system

- Specifies the *minimum essentials* a quality system must include in order to achieve those goals.

Many facilities are pleasantly surprised to discover that their existing quality systems already meet ISO 9000 requirements in many respects. There is, after all, nothing new or radically different in the standard. And the standard emphasizes goals and objectives (as outlined above). It does not prescribe specific strategies, tactics, and procedures. This is what gives ISO 9000 its enormous flexibility.

The Quality Loop

First the standard describes the ideal quality system in graphic form as a quality loop. One version of the loop is for manufacturing (ISO 9004; Fig. 5-1); the other, for service (ISO 9004-2; Fig. 5-2). The qual-

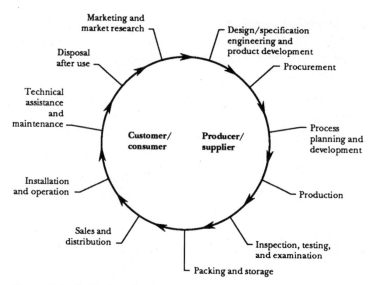

Figure 5-1. Quality loop for ISO 9004.

ity loop includes all stages of the quality system and shows their relationships. Notice that the gathering of customer requirements is a prominent part of these continuous loops.

The technical requirements and recommendations in this section—indeed, throughout this book—all fit neatly into the "quality loop" schematic, creating an effective and dynamic quality system.

Quality System Goals

As noted, the standard's principal intent is to prescribe goals and objectives, not specific tactics. Here, according to the standard, are the goals of the ideal quality system.

The system must be well understood and effective. Understanding is a function of documentation and training, both covered elsewhere in the standard. Effectiveness is self-explanatory, and means for enforcing audits, corrective action, reviews, etc., are also built into the standard, as we shall see.

The system must be effective at achieving quality objectives. This is self-explanatory, and it follows logically from the requirements under

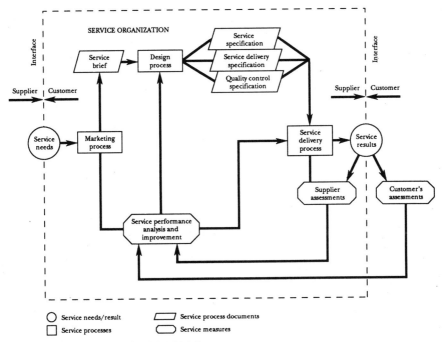

Figure 5-2. Quality loop for ISO 9004-2.

Management Responsibility. Why have a quality system if it does not meet the facility's quality goals?

The system must provide confidence that output actually meets customer expectations. This is usually an automatic "quality objective," but since it is the whole purpose of having a quality system, it is expressed as a separate goal.

The system should give emphasis to preventive actions. At the same time, it should maintain the ability to detect, respond to, and correct failures after they occur. Some managers, pointing to the standard's sections on inspection and related activities, charge that the standard is based on detection. In fact, the standard's true goal, a higher and more logical one, is that *no nonconforming product reach the customer.* The first line of defense against this is prevention, and here the standard makes it clear that the quality system should be based on prevention. But the system must also include detection measures adequate enough to ensure that nonconforming output does not reach customers.

The system must be documented.   This too is based upon logic. Turnover is a fact of life in every facility. Documentation helps ensure continuity. Documentation also aids in training, and ensures that everyone involved in a particular process is "singing from the same page in the hymnal." Documentation exposes weaknesses, trouble spots, and gaps in the quality system. More practically speaking, documentation is essential to the assessing and certifying processes. We will examine quality system documentation in the next chapter.

These are the overriding goals that the quality system is expected to achieve.

Quality System Elements

The ISO 9000 standard and its various models and guidelines are, in fact, blueprints for what ISO considers to be the ideal quality system. Having specified some generic, rather obvious, and quite logical goals for the quality system, the standard goes on to set forth a roster of elements which it considers important for an effective quality system to achieve the ultimate business goal: producing output which meets customer requirements.

However—and this is a crucial point—nowhere does the standard say that these other "elements" are mandatory. The wording of the standard is quite deliberately designed to permit flexibility and judgment on the part of facility management as well as registrars and assessors. The following clauses are important (italics added):

> The quality systems should be structured and *adapted to the company's particular type of business,* and should *take into account* the *appropriate* elements outlined in this International Standard.
> *ISO 9004 (1987), 4.4.3*

> In meeting specified requirements, *timely consideration needs to be given* to the following activities . . .   *ISO 9001 (1987), 4.2 (note)*

Clearly, the standard does not intend to impose requirements of any kind aside from those which it deems essential to achievement of the overriding goal: ensuring that output meets customer requirements. Instead, the sections of the various models describe elements which management should consider including in a quality system. In reality, as we will see throughout this book, many of these elements are essential for the majority of facilities.

It is up to facility management, assisted if necessary by experienced ISO consultants and assessors, to determine the precise shape of the quality system appropriate to the facility's business, marketplace, and objectives. You will find that the ISO 9000 standard is flexible enough to accommodate virtually all.

Quality Costs: ISO 9004.6

Checklist of Requirements

- Operating quality costs and external quality assurance costs should be identified and measured.
- Quality costs should be reported to and monitored by management in the context of other costs and revenues.

Quality in general has a profound effect on the facility's financial health, or lack thereof. The ultimate purpose of any quality program is to maintain and improve the facility's health by satisfying its customers. A valuable way to assess the effectiveness of a quality system is to measure and monitor its costs as well as the return on investment which it generates. For that reason, the standard recommends that two broad categories of quality costs be monitored, analyzed, and reported to management: operating costs and external costs.

Types of Quality Costs

Operating quality costs are the costs incurred to attain and verify necessary quality levels. These include costs of activities intended to prevent quality problems and to assess products, services, and systems for quality problems.

Included in operating quality costs are the costs of failures, which are really the costs of quality problems themselves. Such failure costs can include costs of poor quality detected internally. They also include quality failures in the field, resulting in warranty costs, service costs, and loss of customer goodwill.

External quality costs are the costs of proving the effectiveness of the facility's quality system to others: customers, regulatory groups, certifying bodies, and the like.

Quality Cost Reporting

The standard recommends that quality costs be routinely reported to and monitored by management. Clearly, the standard regards quality cost reporting as an important element of management planning. Suggested uses of quality cost reports include:

1. Evaluate effectiveness of quality system.
2. Pinpoint areas requiring improvement.
3. Establish quality objectives.

Internal Quality Audits: ISO 9001, 4.17; ISO 9004, 5.4; ISO 9004-2, 5.4.4

Checklist of Requirements

- Regular internal audits must be conducted to evaluate how effectively a quality system is achieving stated objectives.
- Audits must be conducted in accordance with an audit plan.
- Audit findings must be documented and acted upon by senior management.

Audits are a major element in an ISO 9000 quality system. Under ISO there are two types of regular external audits as well as a requirement for internal auditing measures.

Facilities registered to one of the contractual models (ISO 9001, 9002, or 9003) undergo initial audits, or assessments, by the registrar. Registered facilities are also subject to semiannual surveillance visits, which can amount to full-scale audits from time to time. We will delve into these types of audits in Chap. 13.

The standard also obligates management to take regular measures to assess the quality system and ensure that it is meeting stated objectives—as required under Management Responsibility. To meet this requirement, the standard suggests that facilities "should" conduct regular internal audits of the quality system.

The Audit Plan

The facility must conduct these internal audits in accordance with a documented plan, which should cover every element of the quality system. The standard suggests that areas for internal audit attention include:

Procedures (documented vs. actual)

Resources

Facilities

Measurement systems and results

Documentation and records

Nonconformances reported in previous audits

The following factors should be spelled out in the facility's audit plan:

- Areas to be audited.
- Frequency of audits. The standard does not mandate frequency. It is up to management to determine when an audit is "appropriate." In practice, it is prudent for every element of the quality system to undergo internal audit no less often than once a year.
- Qualifications of people carrying out audits. Again, these are up to the judgment of facility management; the standard uses the term "competent." It does require that auditors have no involvement in the area(s) being audited.
- Basis for carrying out audits. In addition to timing issues, the plan may call for audits to be triggered by such events as a certain level

of customer complaints, suspect statistical analyses, or excessive nonconformances detected in previous internal audits.

- Procedures for reporting audit findings.

Audit Findings

Audit results should be documented and brought to the attention of the management of audited areas. The standard defines "results" as including nonconformances, suggested corrective actions, and assessments of the effectiveness of corrective actions that were recommended after earlier audits.

Personnel and Training: ISO 9001, 4.18; ISO 9004, 18; ISO 9004-2, 5.3

Checklist of Requirements

- Employees assigned to work affecting quality shall meet established qualification standards based on education, training, and/or experience.
- Facility must have a system that identifies training needs of people whose work affects quality.
- Facility should provide such training where needs exist.
- Facility must maintain training records.
- Facility should strive to motivate all employees toward quality performance.

The ISO 9000 standard recognizes how vital *personnel* are to the success of a quality system. Accordingly, the standard sets forth detailed requirements and guidelines governing qualification, training, and motivation of employees whose work affects quality in any way.

Interestingly, the requirements in the contractual models (ISO 9001, 9002, and 9003) are rather sparse. It is the ISO 9004 guidelines documents that spell out the details.

Employee Qualifications

Some jobs, especially technical ones, are best filled by employees meeting certain formal qualifications. These qualifications may be in the form of certifications, licenses, or demonstration of special skills. The standard advises facilities to have a system for determining what positions fall into this category. In such cases, the facility should implement procedures for verifying that necessary qualifications have been met.

Who Should Undergo Training?

The ISO 9000 standard does not in itself require training of any kind. This is, once again, an area left up to the best judgment of facility management. The standard acknowledges, for example, that many employees may meet the qualifications for their positions by virtue of experience.

However, the standard clearly regards training as a good thing per se. It suggests that facility management consider some form of training for everyone. It makes special mention of people whose work affects quality (of course), as well as new hires and transferees, as logical candidates for training.

What Kind of Training Should Be Provided?

In general, facilities should provide training to employees in accordance with their documented training plan. They should also provide whatever training is required to ensure that employees meet the documented qualifications of their positions. The standard makes more specific suggestions for various employee levels:

- *Management personnel*—quality system understanding
- *Technical personnel*—technical skills needed to meet obligations of the quality plan, as well as statistical techniques
- *Line management and hourly workers*—skills needed to perform assigned tasks and meet obligations of the quality plan, safety, and (potentially) statistical techniques

What Kinds of Motivation Methods Are Required?

In a word, none. That should come as no surprise. The standard does acknowledge that motivational techniques are commonly used in facilities today. It counsels facilities to utilize motivational methods that

- Foster worker involvement
- Emphasize the role of quality in the accomplishment of tasks
- Emphasize the impact of quality on the facility's success
- Recognize and reward efforts which contribute to the success of the quality system

This chapter has outlined the ISO 9000 requirements and guidelines with regard to some basic elements of the facility's quality system. These are very general areas that apply to virtually every quality system. In the next few chapters, we shall look at what the standard has to say about some finer points of the quality system. We will see what it says about quality in subcontractor and customer relationships—and we will explore everyone's favorite topic: documentation.

6

Documenting the Quality System

ISO 9000 is a paperwork nightmare and record storage nightmare.

ISO 9000's high structure and documented system will stifle innovation and initiative—paperwork over all else!
RECENT SEMINAR ATTENDEES

Documentation is central to ISO 9000. And nothing else in ISO 9000 brings out management fear and loathing as strongly as does its emphasis on documentation. Many firms see ISO 9000 as unnecessarily paper-heavy and bureaucratic. Some go so far as to say that ISO 9000 is not about quality at all, but about redundant recordkeeping and paper shuffling.

At first blush, it is easy to understand the concern some have about ISO 9000's documentation requirements. The standard itself is rife with references to documentation. ISO 9001 devotes two sections to it, and refers to documentation and recordkeeping in no fewer than 50 other places. ISO 9004 also devotes two sections to documentation requirements. ISO 9004-2 describes the quality system as consisting of three main elements: the quality loop, internal quality audits, and documentation.

Is the standard's emphasis on documentation and recordkeeping excessive, unnecessary, and burdensome? To answer that question, let us look at the objectives for documentation as set forth by the standard:

> Documentation should ensure a common understanding of quality policies and procedures.   *ISO 9004 (1987), 5.3.1*

> Sufficient documentation should be available to follow the achievement of the required product quality and effective operation of the quality management system.
>   *ISO 9004 (1987), 17.2*

Do these sound onerous or threatening? No. In fact, they sound rather reasonable. Certainly, as any businessperson can attest, some form of documentation and recordkeeping is essential to operating any business.

Consider another statement in the standard:

> Care should be taken to limit documentation to the extent pertinent to the application.   *ISO 9004 (1987), 5.3.1*

ISO 9000, then, *requires* only a reasonable and prudent level of recordkeeping and documentation—and even cautions the facility against overdoing it. Therefore, the facility adopting ISO 9000 need not create redundant recordkeeping or documentation systems. Instead, as we will see in Chap. 12, the facility should approach the matter this way:

- Compare the standard's requirements against its existing operation.
- Adapt existing documentation and recordkeeping systems as necessary to conform to the standard.
- Then, and only then, eliminate any remaining nonconformances with additional documentation and recordkeeping.

The various parts of ISO 9000 describe documentation requirements in several different sections, as examined in detail below:

Documentation of the System

Document Control

Quality Records

Documentation of the System: ISO 9004, 5.3; ISO 9004-2, 5.4.3.1

Checklist of Requirements

- Quality system should be documented in a systematic and orderly manner in the form of written policies and procedures.

- Quality system documentation should be understood, agreed to, and accessible by all personnel whose activities affect quality.

The ISO 9000 quality system is intended to be planned, orderly, controlled, and verifiable. Policies and procedures are necessary to ensure that

- Employees know what to do
- Management maintains control
- Oversight bodies, such as registrars, can attest to the effectiveness of the quality system

Quality system documentation is usually composed of several different levels. The standard describes each of these levels without *mandating* any of them. This is, once again, an area where the standard allows flexibility for application and implementation.

The Quality Manual

The "top tier" of quality system documentation is usually a *quality manual.* Of all the elements which make up the ISO 9000 quality system, none is as central and important as the quality manual. It serves a multitude of essential purposes.

1. It aids in the creation and implementation of the quality system.

2. It describes the objectives and structure of the quality system.

3. It demonstrates management's commitment to the quality system.

4. It serves as a cross-reference between the quality system and the quality system standard to which the facility is certified.

5. It serves as a cross-reference among facility procedures.

6. It serves as quality system reference document for the ISO 9000 registrar as well as other outside entities (such as customers, prospects, and investors) which the facility may designate.

7. It provides an "adequate" description of the quality system.

Since many American firms already have quality manuals, their managers are accustomed to the idea. But "traditional" U.S. quality manuals are strikingly different from the typical ISO 9000 version.

For one thing, the typical American quality manual is huge. The ISO 9000 quality manual, on the other hand, need be 40 or 50 pages long at most. Such compression is achievable because the ISO 9000 quality manual does not recite or detail procedures; it simply makes reference to them.

Another difference is purpose. Too often, American quality manuals are management "wish lists" with little resemblance to actual facility practice. The ISO 9000 is just the reverse: a 1-to-1 reflection of the facility's quality system as it is operated every day.

Contents of the Manual

The standard suggests that methods be established for making changes to the manual and controlling its distribution. But nowhere does the standard prescribe the exact contents. Even the format is left up to the individual facility. But since the usual purpose of the manual is to document the facility's adherence to the ISO 9000 quality system standard, it follows that the manual must address each section of the ISO 9000 model which the facility adopts.

Therefore, if the facility adopts ISO 9001, and its quality system addresses all the elements described all 20 sections of ISO 9001, the manual should also address the requirements of those 20 sections, specifying in general how the quality system conforms. The manual need not be structured in the same order as the standard. But it is often easier to adopt that structure. Whatever system is chosen, the manual must be cross-referenced to each of the 20 sections.

Though the manual may be thought of as the ultimate "procedure" or "work instruction"—and, in many facilities, is actively used as a training and initiation document—it usually does not get as detailed or specific as a procedure. It is, rather, a general document, more philosophical than procedural. It expresses general principles and refers the reader to specific procedures and work instructions as needed.

In addition to the material addressing the standard's requirements, the typical ISO 9000 quality manual often includes the following.

- Brief statement of the facility's quality policy—in compliance with the standard's requirement that the quality policy be publicized to all facility employees
- Brief facility profile—useful when the quality manual is presented to potential customers and suppliers
- Facility mission statement (optional)
- Distribution list (for controlled circulation)
- Centralized list of facility procedures

In addition to playing a vital role in the development and operation of the facility's quality system, the manual is critical to the ISO 9000 certification process. The quality manual is examined in detail in Chap. 12; a sample manual appears in Appendix C.

Quality Plans and Operating Procedures

The second and more detailed tier of quality system documentation relates to plans and operating procedures. There is nothing in the standard that requires the development of these documents per se. However, the standard does call for development of documents when the absence of same would adversely affect quality. As a practical matter, many, if not most, facilities develop some sort of quality plans and/or operating procedures if they are not already in place.

Quality plans are definitional documents, usually tied to specific output (product or service). They describe:

The quality objectives for output

Responsibility and authority for meeting those objectives

Resources required

Sequence of activities, cross-referencing procedures, work instructions (see below)

Quality monitoring methods

Quality characteristics to be monitored

Recordkeeping requirements

Operating procedures are more detailed still. Procedures are specific "how-to's" for carrying out activities outlined in one or more quality plans. They should include cross-references to the related quality plans and, where appropriate, to the quality manual. Operating procedures are not necessarily job descriptions (though they can be developed as such); they are specific to the process, not to an individual.

Many facilities develop quality plans and operating procedures by flowcharting the process, searching for the appropriate areas and then creating the necessary documents along with the associated controls. This network of documents may also include an organization chart in order to ensure that the relationship of process elements, quality system, and documentation is thoroughly understood by all.

Third-Level Documentation

Depending on the facility, there may be levels of quality system documentation beyond quality plans and procedures. Examples include operating instructions, manuals, and books. These levels of documentation are highly specific to individual workers and tasks and, in keeping with ISO's dictum against burdensome documentation, should be kept to a minimum.

Managing Quality System Documentation

As you have discerned, the ISO 9000 standard requires quality system documentation, but qualifies its discussion of documentation with terms such as "should" and "appropriate." In addition, the standard shies away from making hard-and-fast rules on how to generate and use the documentation. Instead, as usual, the standard enumerates goals and guidelines and leaves specifics up to the enlightened wisdom of facility management.

Once again, the goals have a commonsense orientation:

- Procedures and other elements of quality system documentation should be agreed to. These elements, up to and including the quality manual, are best created with the advice and counsel of the people actually doing the work.

- Documentation should be understood—that is, written in straightforward language—and legible. It must also be accessible to the personnel who need it.

Document Control, Quality Records: ISO 9001, 4.5, 4.16; ISO 9004, 17

Checklist of Requirements

- Documents relating to quality system requirements must be created in accordance with documented procedures.

- Personnel whose activities affect quality must have access to current editions of documents pertinent to their quality-related functions.

- Changes to such documents shall be made and approved according to procedures.

According to the standard, quality documentation is composed of drawings, specifications, blueprints, procedures, and many other types of records. All are intended to document the quality level of output as well as the overall performance of the quality system.

The standard outlines a few guidelines for the facility's document control scheme:

- Quality documents, and any subsequent revisions, are to be reviewed and approved by authorized persons.

- Documentation and records should be legible, dated, identifiable, and orderly.

- Current editions of quality documents must be available where needed—that is, where operations affecting quality are being performed.

- Quality records and documentation should be stored in a way to prevent damage, loss, and deterioration.

- Quality documents and records should be retained as long as they are needed to facilitate analysis of quality trends and to determine the necessity for, and effectiveness of, corrective action. These retention periods should be documented.

- To prevent obsolete editions from being used, a procedure must ensure that outdated documents are promptly discarded.

- To preclude further the risk of inadvertently using obsolete editions, a master control list (or some other type of list) must itemize current editions of quality documents.

The ISO standard is dead serious about document control. This is evident in its repeated use of the term "shall" instead of "should." But on the whole, the standard presents *objectives* for the quality system without telling the facility how it must go about achieving those objectives. It requires only that the facility control changes through a documented procedure.

7

Dealing with Subcontractors

Virtually every type of business acquires some form of product or service from outside suppliers. Input ranges from the most basic raw materials, to finished goods of incredible complexity, to a host of intricate service packages. In this era of decentralization, spin-offs, and "sticking to the knitting," vertical integration is clearly out of fashion. Businesses depend upon outside suppliers more than ever. Many are, in fact, virtual hostages to them.

This locked-in dependency has a critical impact on quality. As quality gurus have counseled for many years, the quality of a process's output—product or service—begins with the quality of the process's input—the products or services supplied to it.

The quality of input has a direct and measurable impact on the scope, rigor, and effectiveness of the facility's quality system. In other words, the higher the quality of the input, the less extensive the facility's quality measures have to be. Moreover, excellent input almost by definition improves the quality of output.

Optimally, the input should be of such consistently high quality that the facility can incorporate it into its process upon arrival, without any inspection or other measures. The resulting economies can be exponential, including:

- Zero inspection costs
- Lower inventory costs (just-in-time delivery)

- Less variability in critical characteristics, improving quality at each stage of the process

On the other hand, an ineffective supplier system—typified by multiple or redundant suppliers, emphasis on bidding wars, and adversarial relationships—puts excruciating pressure on the facility's quality system and virtually guarantees a consistently lower level quality of output.

The ISO 9000 quality system standard recognizes the vital impact that suppliers, or *subcontractors,* have on a facility's quality system. Its requirements for subcontractor relationships are based upon a philosophy of open and close communication between facility and subcontractor. These guidelines are meant to create clear understanding of requirements on both sides. An ISO 9000 procurement system has two stated outcomes, with obvious benefits to both sides:

1. Creation of continual improvement between supplier and subcontractor

2. Avoidance or quick settlement of quality disputes

The requirements and guidelines are presented under two topic headings:

Purchasing

Quality in Procurement

For our purposes, these can be explored in a single discussion.

Purchasing, Quality in Procurement: ISO 9001, 4.6; ISO 9004, 9; ISO 9004-2, 6.2.4.3

Checklist of Requirements

- Procurement of input should be planned and controlled.
- Facility should establish a close working relationship and feedback system with each subcontractor.

- Facility should establish measures for controlling input.
- Facility should maintain appropriate records.

Procurement Control System

Procurement control requirements are quite similar to the quality system requirements outlined elsewhere in the standard. They follow the ISO 9000 principles of planning, control, and documentation.

The first and most important requirement is that the facility establish a close working relationship and feedback system with each subcontractor. Within this overall requirement exists an array of others. The standard tempers these passages with the word "should." It also refers to these guidelines as "minimum."

1. *Subcontractors should demonstrate capability of meeting requirements.* Before ordering from a subcontractor, it is only good common sense to make sure that the subcontractor has the ability to meet the facility's needs. The standard requires the facility to use a system for verifying subcontractor capability. This system may include:

- On-site assessment of subcontractor's capability and/or quality system
- Prior history with same or similar input
- Evaluation and testing of sample input
- Published experience of other users

The standard also suggests that the facility request subcontractor certification to one of the ISO models (ISO 9001, 9002, or 9003) as a strategy for meeting this requirement.

2. *Requirements should be clearly defined—and understood.* The facility and subcontractor should define and agree upon the crucial characteristics of the input to be provided. These characteristics are usually set forth in one or more standard documents, such as purchase orders, accompanied by blueprints, drawings, specification sheets, and other supporting materials. It is up to the facility to ensure that all vital details are communicated to *and understood by* the subcontractor.

Therefore, the standard suggests that the facility employ procedures governing the measures necessary to attain the required level of understanding. These procedures may involve creation and verification of purchase orders and supporting documents, arrangement and management of facility/subcontractor meetings, and other measures, "as appropriate."

3. *Facility and subcontractor should agree on the degree of quality assurance that subcontractor is to provide.* An array of options is available here:

- None. The facility conducts 100 percent inspection of input.
- Subcontractor conducts inspection and testing (100 percent or through lot sampling), providing test results to facility.
- Subcontractor provides various process control records, including inspection and test data, with shipments.
- Facility relies on subcontractor quality assurance without verification.

4. *Facility and subcontractor should agree on methods of verifying conformance.* The facility should ensure that the subcontractor clearly understands how the facility will verify that input conforms to requirements. Such understanding will smooth communication and reduce disputes. To fulfill this requirement, the facility may have to implement formal procedures. The facility and subcontractor may wish to exchange technical data with other subcontractors, and engage in joint training in various statistical techniques and improvement methods.

5. *Facility and subcontractor should agree on systems and procedures for dealing with routine and nonroutine matters, especially disputes, affecting quality.* This is a simple matter of arranging for open channels of communication between the facility and the subcontractor.

Controlling Input

The ISO 9000 standard is very specific about the facility's obligation to control (1) materials of any nature that are known to be nonconforming to requirements and (2) materials whose conformance status is unknown. In essence, the standard requires the facility to make certain, by means of documented procedures, that such materials remain separate from conforming materials.

This obligation applies to input in general. The standard requires that the procedure for receiving input be "carefully planned." Basically, the procedure should ensure that received input is controlled and kept separate until its conformance status has been determined.

If input is "accepted" (by means of subcontractor certification or other means) prior to receipt, then this requirement may be moot. But many facilities employ a receiving inspection procedure. Those that do are admonished to "bear cost in mind" when developing their inspection system. The standard also requires such facilities to

- Select inspection characteristics carefully
- Ensure that inspections are carried out by trained and qualified personnel using inspection instruments that are properly calibrated

Quality Records

As with most aspects of the quality system standard, facilities are obligated to maintain quality records of their subcontractor activities. The standard specifically mentions records containing historical data that aid in assessing supplier performance and evaluating quality trends.

8

Dealing with Customers

American managers who are implementing ISO 9000 quality systems often make the same beleaguered comment: "ISO 9000 doesn't address customer satisfaction."

It is easy to see how some would reach this erroneous conclusion. The contractual models—ISO 9001, 9002, and 9003—have no sections dedicated to customers per se. However, ISO 9004 and 9004-2—the guidelines documents for manufacturing and service applications—devote extensive attention to the role of customers in the facility's quality system. Both versions of the quality loop include customers as an element (see Figs. 5-1 and 5-2). In fact, both versions "begin" and "end" with customers.

That schematic attests to the importance ISO 9000 places upon customers in the development and management of the facility's quality system. The requirements and guidelines are presented among a number of topic headings, all explored in detail below:

Quality in Marketing

Interface with Customers

Contract Review

Purchaser-Supplied Product

Servicing

Quality in Marketing: ISO 9004, 7; ISO 9004-2, 6.1

Checklist of Requirements

- Marketing establishes quality requirements for output.
- Marketing creates the product (or service) brief.
- Marketing operates an information monitoring and feedback system to evaluate customer requirements.

In most organizations, marketing is the main interface between the facility and the customer. Recognizing this, ISO 9000 places upon marketing the responsibility for:

- Identifying customer requirements
- Translating these requirements into initial product or service specifications
- Translating product or service features into advertising
- Gathering, analyzing, and communicating customer feedback

When appropriate, facilities should have systems and procedures for carrying out these activities.

Identifying Customer Requirements

According to the ISO 9000 standard, marketing is responsible for identifying customer requirements—including, of course, all requirements with respect to quality. But the responsibility goes well beyond that. Marketing must also take the lead in the following areas:

- Determining the need for products or services
- Defining the market for products or services
- Determining and evaluating competitive offerings and legal or regulatory issues, if any
- Defining the details of customer needs and expectations, including implicit and/or unstated needs and expectations
- Identifying specific quality requirements and characteristics

These activities should be conducted, not just in the initial development phase, but also on an ongoing basis for existing products or services.

Creating the Product Brief

Marketing should, by procedure, create a *product brief* which formally summarizes its findings with respect to product or service features, especially as they relate to quality. The product brief is, in effect, a preliminary set of specifications which marketing communicates to other areas of the facility. It should expressly relate these specifications to the facility's internal capabilities.

The product brief is used as the basis for designing the facility's product or service (see Chap. 9). It leads to the development of formal (and more detailed) specifications and quality characteristics. These characteristics act as a baseline or benchmark against which the resulting output can be measured.

The specifics of the product brief can, of course, vary tremendously from facility to facility. The standard makes no specific requirements; it includes only areas for consideration, such as:

- Performance and sensory characteristics
- Statutory or regulatory requirements
- Installation and use issues
- Packaging
- Quality control and quality assurance factors

Advertising

ISO 9004-2, the guidelines document for service functions, makes specific mention of quality in advertising. It calls for a facility to see to it that its advertising:

- Reflects the product or service specifications
- Takes into account customers' perception of quality
- Refrains from offering exaggerated or unsubstantiated claims

At present these guidelines appear only in the service document, but facilities conforming to ISO 9001, 9002, or 9003 and ISO 9004 would do well to conform to the service guidelines as well.

Customer Feedback

Finally, marketing is responsible for "closing the customer loop" by operating a continuous information monitoring and feedback system. The system should operate in accordance with defined procedures, focusing specifically on feedback relating to the quality of output. This information should be communicated to appropriate departments of the facility.

The information should be used for the following purposes:

- To determine customers' quality experience as compared with quality expectations
- To identify potential output improvements
- To serve as part of the continuous evaluation of customer requirements called for above

Interface with Customers: ISO 9004-2, 5.5

Checklist of Requirements

- Management should establish and regularly review methods of interaction between facility and customer.

The Customer Interface section of the service document expands on some of the themes of the marketing guidelines described above. While these provisions do not appear at present in other parts of the standard, they are well worth incorporating, as appropriate, into every quality system.

The rationale for this section is simply that every interface between facility and customer is important. The "reality" of these interactions, says the standard, contributes to how the customer views the facility. The inference is that the health of the facility is directly related to the health of the "quality image" held by its customers.

The facility should recognize this by

- Instituting procedures to make sure that interactions with customers are as effective as possible
- Routinely reviewing methods of promoting customer contact

This section of the standard also discusses the importance of effective communication with customers. Difficulties in communication should be given prompt attention, especially when they involve issues such as:

- Product or service features, benefits, availability, and cost
- Service and warranty issues
- Customer needs and expectations

Contract Review:
ISO 9001, 4.3

Checklist of Requirements

- Facility shall maintain procedures for conducting and documenting contract reviews.

This section of ISO 9001, which also appears in ISO 9002 and 9003, has strong parallels to the Quality in Marketing requirements discussed above. Since these requirements pertain to contractual relationships, they are restated much more pithily in the context of a "contract" between facility and customer.

The Contract Review section obligates the facility to maintain procedures for evaluating customer requirements and comparing them with the facility's capabilities. The reviews must ensure that:

- Requirements are adequately defined and documented
- Requirements are within facility capabilities
- Discrepancies are resolved

As might be expected, this section also requires that the facility maintain records of all contract reviews.

Purchaser-Supplied
Product: ISO 9001, 4.7

Checklist of Requirements

- Facility shall maintain procedures to control and protect materials provided to it by customers or purchasers.

This section of ISO 9001, which appears also in ISO 9002 and 9003, applies only to a special category of facility. This is a facility which, as part of its process, receives materials, products, or services owned by customers (purchasers) for inclusion in the output which is then supplied to those purchasers.

For example, a book manufacturer (supplier) is in the business of printing and binding books for sale to a book publisher (purchaser). As part of the process, the publisher supplies the book manufacturer with a computer disk containing the text which is to be included in the final output. That disk is *purchaser-supplied product.*

Facilities which receive such purchaser-supplied product (or service) must monitor and secure it at each point during which it is under the facility's control.

The system maintained by the facility should:

- Document suitability of the product or service for the intended purpose, via inspection or other means
- Keep purchaser-supplied product or service safe and secure
- Report to the purchaser any occurrences of nonconformance, shrinkage, damage, etc., affecting the purchaser-supplied product or service

Servicing: ISO 9001, 4.19

Checklist of Requirements

- Facility shall maintain procedures to ensure that contractually required servicing is performed according to requirements.

At 24 words, Servicing is the second shortest section in the ISO standards. (See Statistical Techniques in Chap. 10 for number one.)

It appears only in ISO 9001 and usually applies solely to facilities whose customer contracts oblige them (by warranty or other means) to provide postsale servicing.

This section obligates the supplier to establish and maintain procedures for performing all contractual service and verifying that the service meets specified requirements. Servicing requirements may include customer use documentation, installation instructions, postsale support facilities (with staff and equipment), and field measuring and test equipment.

When postsale servicing is part of a customer contract, the facility's product design function must anticipate service requirements with appropriate procedures, mechanisms, personnel, and skills, and ensure that these are in place well in advance of initial deliveries. An "early-warning system" should be in place to ensure timely detection of service needs.

9

Designing and Producing the Output

So far, we have looked at what ISO 9000 says about the components of the quality system, its documentation, and relations with subcontractors and customers. These elements of the quality system standard are general and external. They do not directly address the output (product or service) being produced.

Still, these elements are critical to the success of other, output-specific provisions of the standard. Ultimately, they are quite critical to the quality of the output itself. They are what makes ISO 9000 a quality *system* standard, embracing every aspect of the facility which affects the quality of output—as opposed to being a "quality tool" or "technique," which focuses on quality of output only.

ISO has plenty to say about output, though. Having covered these broader issues, we can narrow the focus a bit. This chapter and the two that follow explore the quality system elements required for the creation of output: designing it, producing it, controlling it, and, withal, ensuring its quality.

Facilities which design and produce output, and intend to become certified to ISO 9000, adhere to the 20 sections of ISO 9001 and the associated guidelines in ISO 9004. Facilities which produce output designed by others adhere to the 18 sections of ISO 9002.

The ISO 9000 standard recognizes the critical impact of the design function on the quality of output. Its requirements spell out an integrated, documented, and controlled design process. This process translates the customer requirements listed in the marketing brief (see Chap. 8) into technical specifications and designs which ensure output that meets those requirements. The ISO 9000 design process

- Stays in touch with customer requirements
- Takes into account the capability of the process
- Incorporates identifiable and measurable quality characteristics
- Specifies acceptance criteria and measurement methods for those quality characteristics
- Builds in quality control mechanisms
- Remains adaptable to controlled, disciplined change

The ISO 9000 quality system dovetails this design process to a production process which is planned, controlled, and documented at every juncture. Adherence to the standard results in a design and production process that

- Creates output consistent with customer expectations
- Takes into account pertinent safety and product liability issues
- Generates a predictable return on investment
- Includes systems for managing change, whether internally or externally driven

The various parts of ISO 9000 describe quality system requirements for design and production in several different sections, as explored in detail below:

Design Process/Design Control
Process Control
Product Safety and Liability

Design Process/Design Control: ISO 9001, 4.4; ISO 9004, 8.0; ISO 9004-2, 6.2 (selected)

Checklist of Requirements

- Management should establish a design program appropriate to the application, complexity, and innovation of the output.

- Management must see to it that the design function is aware of quality responsibilities and goals.

- The design process should create technical specifications which result in output that meets customer requirements, safety and environmental regulations, and facility return-on-investment objectives.

- Designs should unambiguously specify quality characteristics, measurement and test methods, and acceptance criteria

- The design process should include objective and periodic design reevaluations and systematic and critical design reviews at prescribed intervals

- The design process should end with a readiness review to verify that all elements deemed necessary for quality production and distribution are in place

- Quality system should include documented procedures for processing, in a controlled manner, routine and emergency design changes throughout the life cycle of the output.

The Design Program

The standard includes a basic and quite obvious requirement that the design program be "time phased"—that is, planned and disciplined, consistent with the application, complexity, and innovation of the output. In other words, the newer, riskier, less standard, and less derivative the output concept is, the more planned, deliberate, and reflective the design process should be.

Design of services should define the service itself, the delivery of the service, and the quality procedures for controlling service characteristics.

Design Personnel

Management is responsible for delegating design responsibility to specific people or entities. This requirement may seem obvious, but it is the standard's way of reinforcing the concept that the design process should be a planned and disciplined one.

The standard also requires management to keep the design function aware of its responsibilities for quality. This reiteration of the Management Responsibility section serves to underline the standard's position: that the design process has a powerful and definitive effect upon quality. In fact, the ISO 9004-2 service document clearly states that "*prevention* of service defects at this stage is less costly than *correction* during service delivery."

Technical Specifications

According to the standard, the chief goal of the design process is to translate customer requirements into technical specifications for output. These specifications should provide "clear and definitive" instructions for

- Quality aspects of the design
- Characteristics important to quality
- Data for procurement from subcontractors
- Instructions for performance of work
- Guidelines for verifying conformance to requirements
- Contingency plans

In all of the above, the design function is cautioned to take into account any pertinent legal, regulatory, and environmental considerations.

Output Testing and Measurement

Just as designs must specify quality aspects and characteristics, so they must specify how the facility will monitor the results of its efforts to maximize the quality of these characteristics. The standard states that measurement methods and acceptance criteria for all quality characteristics should be clearly specified during both design and production phases.

The standard recommends that design ensure the monitoring of quality characteristics by including, for each:

- Tolerances, attributes, and target values
- Measurement and test methods and equipment
- Acceptance and rejection criteria

Design Qualification, Validation, and Review

To ensure that the design process is a rigorously disciplined one, and results in designs that conform to customer requirements, the ISO standard recommends a regular regimen of review activities.

One of these is a *design qualification and validation* process. This process, to be conducted at "significant stages" of the design and development cycle, subjects prototypes, samples, and the like to appropriate tests. These tests may study issues such as:

- Performance, durability, and safety
- Conformance of design features to design goals
- Reverification of original calculations

A broader type of analysis is the *design review*. These reviews are, according to the standard, "formal, documented, systematic, and critical" examinations of design results. They consider, in detail, three major design elements:

- Factors affecting customer needs and satisfaction
- Factors affecting output specification and service requirements
- Factors affecting process specifications and service requirements

The purpose of design reviews is to spot problem areas and initiate corrective actions. The principal objective is, once again, to ensure that the final design meets customer requirements.

The standard calls for regular reviews to be conducted after each significant phase of design development. The final review, at the conclusion of the design process, is documented, as appropriate, with final specifications, drawings, or (in the case of a service) delivery procedures.

This "final" design acts as a baseline against which resulting output is compared. It should undergo review and approval at appropriate management levels. Finally, it should be accompanied by a *market readiness review* to verify that required production capability, field resources, and other support systems are in place to handle the output.

Design Changes

Design changes are a fact of life. Design changes—or, more precisely, inefficient means for handling them—are also a major cause of bloated development costs, competitive shortfalls, extended cycle times, and ultimately loss of share. Deficient design change procedures can also have a devastating effect upon quality and upon the facility's efforts to meet customer requirements.

Under ISO 9000, the facility must have a procedure for controlling the release, change, and use of documents that define the *product baseline*—namely, the final design and/or service specification. Design changes are, in fact, changes to the product baseline. The standard calls this process "configuration management," and intends for it to be planned and disciplined as well.

The procedures should provide for:

- Appropriate approvals
- Scheduled activities for planning and implementing changes
- Updating of documents, work instructions, and other materials, and removal of obsolete documents
- Follow-up to ensure that all specified activities have been carried out

Configuration management procedures are expected to be adequate to handle emergency changes needed to ensure that output conforms to customer requirements.

Design Requalification

The standard recognizes what is, after all, a fact of life: things change. Today's ideal design, even one developed under an ISO 9000 quality system, may be grossly inferior tomorrow. Certainly, competitive pressure and changing markets will result in changing customer expectations. Designs must change too, if the facility is to continue to meet the primary quality goal of satisfying customer expectations.

So ISO 9000 calls for facilities to conduct regular *design requalification reviews* to ensure that the design still meets customer requirements. These reviews should take into account

Field experience

Surveys, research, other customer feedback

Competitive analysis

New technologies

The findings of design requalification reviews can result in routine or emergency design changes, process changes, or new output development initiatives.

Documentation

Finally, the standard requires that all design verification and review activities be given appropriate documentation.

Process Control: ISO 9001 4.9; ISO 9004 10, 11; ISO 9004-2, 6.3

Checklist of Requirements

- Production capability should be monitored, especially those aspects affecting quality, to ensure that production can meet quality requirements.

- Input materials, input processes, and production equipment should be maintained, controlled, and verified, as appropriate, to ensure consistent conformance to requirements.

- Production, especially aspects affecting quality, should be carried out under planned, controlled, and documented conditions.

- Activities to verify quality status should be conducted at critical intervals on a planned and documented basis.

- Special controls and procedures should be implemented for processes which are highly critical to quality and/or difficult to monitor effectively.

- Procedures for making process changes should be thoroughly planned, documented, monitored, and evaluated.

- All quality documentation pertaining to production should be maintained in accordance with documented procedures.

Production Capability

It may seem stunningly obvious, but each production process has a limited level of capability. A process forced to perform beyond its capability is not a "quality" process creating quality output. It is, in fact, a sign of management ignorance.

Under ISO 9000, the capability of a process to produce output to specification is defined and understood at all times. Management is required to implement procedures delimiting general capability. Design Requirements sections address this issue, and it is also examined here under Quality in Production.

In addition to general capability, the standard obligates management to identify process operations specifically concerned with output quality. The capability of these operations must be closely monitored to ensure that quality goals are met. The standard also obligates management to "encourage" efforts to develop new methods for improving quality and process capability.

Production Materials and Equipment

The subcontractor sections of the ISO 9000 standard address the control of supplied input. Here, under Production Materials and

Equipment, the standard mentions "auxiliary" input items (such as utilities) and the environment. The standard calls for such factors to be controlled and verified if they are shown to have an impact upon quality.

The same principles and requirements apply to materials and equipment used in production. The standard requires that these be

- Verified as conforming to specifications and quality standards before they are introduced into the process
- Maintained and used under planned and controlled conditions, with traceability if needed
- Subject to regular reverification procedures, including appropriate preventive maintenance

Production Control

As with virtually everything else in an ISO 9000 quality system, production is expected to be planned, controlled, and documented.

1. Planning ensures the appropriate manner and sequence of production.
2. Control covers all aspects of production: materials, equipment, procedures, personnel, supplies, environment, and more.
3. Documentation is essential—but only "to the necessary extent."

Specifically, the standard calls for the use of "documented work instructions." These should, when appropriate, govern production activities which have an impact upon quality. Common work instructions, covering identical activities throughout the facility, can be utilized. Specialized work instructions applying to specific process steps can also be implemented.

Work instructions should

- Describe criteria for determining satisfactory work
- Define work standards
- Be controlled in accordance with document control procedures (see Chap. 6)

Verifying Quality

To minimize errors and maximize production, verification of quality status—not only of output, but also of process elements affecting output quality—should be ascertained "at important points" in the production sequence.

The verification requirement specifically refutes a common criticism of ISO 9000: that it is "inspection based." ISO 9000 does not "require" inspection; it does not even prefer inspection. It requires verification of quality status via process control methods, including control charts and statistical sampling procedures and plans. If such controls are not feasible or practical, then product control methods, such as inspection, must be employed.

The standard discourages petty or frivolous verification systems by stating that verifications should relate directly to either finished output specifications or to some internal process requirement. Verification requirements are examined in further detail in the next chapter.

Special Processes

The standard calls for special measures to be employed to manage quality in certain process areas. These are processes in which

- Output characteristics cannot be measured easily or economically
- Results cannot be fully verified by inspection or testing
- Defects can be detected only after output is in use

The implicit requirement is that management take steps to identify just what these processes are, and the quality issues associated with them. Then, to manage quality in these special processes, the standard suggests that the quality system consider employing intensified quality measures, including:

- Measurement instruments that provide higher accuracy and less variability
- Higher qualification standards, training regimens, and (possibly) certification requirements for employees

■ Specialized physical environments to increase conduciveness to quality

Process Changes

Just as designs undergo change, so do processes. And like design changes, process changes can be chaotic or smooth. As you might expect, ISO 9000 comes down firmly on the side of smooth. Accordingly, the standard calls for process changes to be controlled as follows:

1. Responsibility (i.e., management) should be clearly designated.
2. The customer should be consulted, if appropriate.
3. Implementation should be conducted in accordance with defined procedures.
4. Changes should be documented.

Further, under ISO 9000, process changes must be square-ended with procedures to evaluate subsequent output in order to ensure that the changes have not adversely affected critical characteristics.

Product Safety and Liability: ISO 9004, 19

Checklist of Requirements

■ Facility should identify all safety aspects of the quality of output.

■ Facility should incorporate applicable safety standards into output design, test output for effectiveness of safety measures, and test all user communications for clarity and accuracy.

■ Facility should institute output traceability to ensure effective recall if safety is subsequently found to have been compromised.

Safety and product liability are crucial and volatile issues, especially in today's litigious business environment. Every facility wants to maximize the safety of its customers, obey safety regulations, and minimize exposure to product liability actions.

When safety and product liability are factors, the ISO 9000 quality system standard treats them as a special category of critical quality characteristics. Facilities for which safety is an issue and/or those which are subject to safety regulations of any type are expected to

- Know what the safety issues and regulations are
- Address them with appropriate specifications throughout the design process
- Test for them as part of ongoing verification activities
- Document all safety actions

Facilities are also advised to institute traceability measures in order to recall any output which, subsequent to delivery, is suspected of nonconformance to safety standards. Traceability is discussed in more detail in Chap. 11.

10
Ensuring the Quality of Output

Now we reach the core of the ISO 9000 quality system. The requirements covered in earlier chapters set the stage; here we will examine what the standard says about ensuring the quality of output as it moves through the process.

There is nothing revolutionary in these technical requirements. Like the rest of the ISO 9000 standard, the guidelines in this area are mainly good common sense. The approach differs somewhat between the service and the nonservice parts of the standard, but the essential strategy is the same:

1. Know what the critical quality characteristics and acceptance standards are.

2. Verify conformance to standards at critical process points.

3. Utilize procedures to ensure adequacy and accuracy of measuring equipment.

4. Maintain appropriate identification of verification status of output at all points.

5. Utilize appropriate statistical techniques.

6. Identify output appropriately.

7. Segregate nonconforming output.

8. Determine causes of nonconformances.

9. Devise, implement, and verify corrective actions.

The last four provisions are examined in Chap. 11. The provisions we will look at here are worded more specifically—but not much more—than other parts of the standard. But they remain deftly phrased and generally applicable. It is the genius of the ISO 9000 standard that it can be adapted and applied to such a broad range of products and services.

Notice that the strategy described above is, in fact, a cyclical prescription for *continuous improvement*. ISO 9000 is not a system for sorting acceptable output from defective output. It is a system to ensure that (1) customers receive output which meets their criteria and (2) process elements which do not contribute to that goal are constantly improved.

The process of creating services is much different from the process of creating products. As a result, ISO 9004 (products) and ISO 9004-2 (services) differ rather significantly. So in the first section of this chapter we will focus on the service quality guidelines discussed in ISO 9004-2. The remaining sections will take up the product quality requirements outlined in ISO 9004 as well as in ISO 9001 (the contractual model).

Even if your facility is strictly involved with products, you should review the requirements of the service section of the standard, since they are much more aggressive regarding corrective action and continuous improvement. In real life, almost no facility is so purely into "making products" that it can successfully ignore quality service. In fact, it can be argued that a product company cannot succeed on the quality of its output alone. Without quality service to go with it, the company is doomed to fail.

ISO 9000 describes quality system requirements for ensuring the quality of output in several different sections, as explored in detail below:

Quality in the Production of Services

Inspection and Testing

Inspection, Measuring, and Test Equipment

Inspection and Test Status

Statistical Techniques

Quality in the Production of Services: ISO 9004-2 6.3, 6.4

Checklist of Requirements

- Services should be delivered according to a documented specification.

- The service delivery process should undergo a continuous assessment at critical process points, using documented and verified measurement and testing methods.

- The service delivery process should aggressively collect and analyze customer assessments of service quality.

- Nonconformities should be recorded and analyzed and then subjected to appropriate, documented, corrective action.

- Management should operate a system to gather data on service performance and analyze it for deficiencies, corrective actions, and opportunities for improvement.

- Management should operate a program for continuously improving service quality.

Service Specification

The service requirement echoes the Management Responsibility guidelines discussed earlier. Management is expected to define and document the service delivery process. Appropriate personnel should be assigned specific responsibilities—including delivering the process, assessing its effectiveness, obtaining feedback, and performing corrective actions.

Assessment of Service Quality (Internal)

The service delivery process should include quality control procedures at critical process points. These procedures should include:

- Monitoring of key process activities—particularly by personnel delivering the service—to detect deficiencies and ensure customer satisfaction

■ Definitive quality assessment by facility personnel at customer interface, for later comparison with customer quality assessment

Throughout, the system should employ documented and verified measurement and testing methods.

Assessment of Service Quality (Customer)

The standard calls customer assessment "the ultimate measure of the quality of a service." However, objective customer assessment is not easy to obtain. Passive methods, such as reliance upon customer complaints, are not reliable. Customers can be dissatisfied to the point of taking their business elsewhere, without bothering to complain. Effective corrective action is impossible without ongoing, objective gathering of customer assessments of quality.

So the standard calls upon facilities to operate an ongoing system to assess and measure customer satisfaction. The system should study not only how well the service delivery meets the requirements of the service procedure, but also how well the documented service procedure, or *service brief,* meets prevailing customer needs. A facility may carry out its documented service delivery procedures faithfully and believe, therefore, that it is delivering flawless quality; but the customer will not see it that way if the service delivery process does not fully address customer needs.

Elements of this system include:

■ Gathering of positive as well as negative feedback

■ Assessment of the likelihood of future business

■ Comparison of customer assessment with facility's own assessment

Corrective Action

Corrective action is the standard's vehicle for "continuous improvement." It is specified in the product-oriented standards (ISO 9004), but is more thoroughly explained in the service section.

First, the standard sets another Management Responsibility guideline. The quality system should define responsibility and authority for corrective action. Further, ISO 9000 asserts, every individual in the organization is responsible for

- Identifying nonconforming services
- Reporting nonconforming services
- Doing so before customers are affected, if at all possible

Once nonconformances are recorded and analyzed, corrective action should be taken. The standard describes two levels of corrective action:

1. Immediate action should be taken to satisfy customer needs.
2. Longer-term action is called for to identify causes, formulate and implement corrections, and monitor for effectiveness.

Service Performance Analysis and Improvement

At this point, the standard goes beyond process-oriented quality control and corrective action. It sets forth guidelines for assuring continuous improvement of service delivery processes.

The basis for this strategy is effective data collection and analysis. The activity should be undertaken (no surprise) in accordance with a systematic documented procedure, and performed by personnel definitively assigned to the tasks by management. Data should be gathered from all "relevant" sources, including

Internal assessments (quality control)

External assessments (all forms of customer feedback)

Quality audits (external and internal)

Collected data should be used to uncover systemic problems, identify causes, and create effective correction and prevention strategies. The standard calls for the use of modern statistical methods in these activities.

ISO 9000 also calls for the quality system to take aggressive, outward-looking actions to find ways to improve quality. These include:

- Identifying service characteristics whose improvement would most benefit the customer
- Detecting changing market trends
- Finding ways to reduce costs while maintaining or improving service quality

Throughout, management is encouraged to seek input from all personnel in the organization, and to recognize and reward their participation.

Inspection and Testing: ISO 9001 4.10; ISO 9004, 12

Checklist of Requirements

- Quality system must verify conformance to requirements at critical process points.
- Verification methods must be documented and the results recorded in accordance with procedures.
- Output exempted from verification should be made traceable in case of recall.

The title of this section may suggest that ISO 9000 mandates or requires inspection and testing. This is not the case. In no way does the standard require inspection of any kind.

The standard does mandate that the facility verify conformance to requirements at each critical stage of the process. These stages include:

Input

Process points crucial to quality

Output

The method of verification is left up to the facility and, according to the standard, depends on such factors as:

Impact on quality

State of control

Impact on cost

Many facilities meet the verification requirements by implementing inspection and testing procedures. The standard refers specifically to set-up inspections, operator inspections, fixed inspection stations, and roving inspections.

But the wording also allows for alternatives, as long as they are reasonable, proven, and documented. For supplied product, for example, ISO 9000 acknowledges the sufficiency of quality control at the source, so long as evidence of the effectiveness of such control is documented. The standard also acknowledges the efficacy of, and in fact encourages the use of, various within-process monitoring and other control methods.

Some form of completed product verification must be conducted to ensure that output conforms to quality requirements. When appropriate, these verifications may include references to purchase orders to confirm that specific customer requirements are met.

Whatever procedures the facility uses to verify conformance to requirements—whether inspection and testing or other means—the standard requires that they be spelled out in a quality plan or some other form of documentation. These documented procedures must be carried out consistently, and appropriate records must be maintained.

ISO 9000 recognizes that there are times when verification procedures must be waived. In these cases, the facility is obligated to ensure that such items are identified and made traceable in the event recall is subsequently needed.

Inspection, Measuring, and Test Equipment: ISO 9001, 4.11; ISO 9004, 13

Checklist of Requirements

- Devices employed to assess conformance to requirements should be selected and controlled so as to preserve confidence in the integrity of measurements.

- Devices must be calibrated in accordance with documented procedures.

- Output assessed by devices that are found to be nonconforming should be controlled and reassessed in accordance with documented procedures.

The section title notwithstanding, the standard does not require the use of inspection, measuring, and test equipment. What it does require is that the facility exercise *control* over the means used to perform measurements and analyses. Control must be sufficient to ensure confidence in decisions made on the basis of measurements.

Specifically, devices used in obtaining measurements must be appropriate to the task, used by people with appropriate training, and maintained in accordance with requirements. Such devices may include:

Gauges, instruments, and sensors

Special test equipment

Related computer software

Jigs, fixtures, and process instrumentation

The standard sets forth the following guidelines concerning such devices.

- Equipment must be appropriate with respect to specified requirements, capable of required accuracy and precision in the environment in which it will be used, and handled in a way that preserves its functional integrity. Margin for error must be identified.

- Equipment and facilities associated with inspection and test operations must be protected from adjustments which alter calibration.

- Equipment must be calibrated at scheduled intervals, or before use, in accordance with documented procedures. Calibration must ensure that equipment is consistent with a nationally recognized standard or, in the absence of same, with some other documented basis for comparison. Calibration status must be identified by an indicator and documented in records.

Here, the standard also imposes a corrective action obligation. When a device is found to be out of calibration, the facility must follow a procedure to determine the cause of the problem and take remedial action. The facility must also reevaluate previous work affected by the device for conformance to requirements.

Inspection and Test Status: ISO 9001, 4.12; ISO 9004, 11.7

Checklist of Requirements

- Throughout the process, conformance status of output should be identifiable via some documented means.
- The conformance status method should provide traceability to verification activity.
- Verification authority should be documented.

One overriding quality goal of ISO 9000 is to ensure that the only output reaching customers is output which conforms to requirements. Accordingly, the facility must be able to distinguish between conforming and nonconforming product not only after the final verification point but also at each "critical checkpoint" in the process.

As the determination is made regarding which output conforms (hopefully the vast majority) and which does not, the standard requires that the outcome of testing and inspection—conforming vs. nonconforming status—be clearly identified. Such identification can be effected by means of physical marking, records (hard copy or software), physical location, "or other suitable means."

The standard also suggests that the system for determining inspection and test status provide traceability to the verification point where the distinction was made. Records must be kept of the authority responsible for releasing conforming output.

Statistical Techniques: ISO 9001, 4.20; ISO 9004, 20

Checklist of Requirements

- The quality system should include procedures for identifying statistical techniques used in assessing process capability and output characteristics.

At 23 words, Statistical Techniques is the shortest section in ISO 9001. That is not to say that ISO 9000 does not believe in the importance of statistical methods. On the contrary: ISO 9004 states bluntly that they are important to all stages in the quality loop, not just to production or inspection phases. Though the standard does not require their use, it attests to their importance in the improvement of quality, productivity, efficiency, communications, and planning.

The standard obligates the facility to have procedures for identifying statistical techniques for verifying the acceptability of process capability and product characteristics. These procedures should be employed in all areas where their use will demonstrably improve quality—such as process control, process capability, inspection planning, and defect analysis. In addition, the standard suggests that statistical techniques be considered for nonproduction areas. Candidates here include market analysis, design, and performance assessment.

The standard does not mandate any particular statistical techniques. Suggestions for consideration include design of experiments/factorial analysis, variance/regression analysis, safety evaluation/risk analysis, cusum techniques, and statistical sampling inspection. Facilities are free to investigate and implement other statistical techniques which are shown to contribute to quality objectives.

11

Controlling and Improving Output

This final phase in our examination of technical requirements closes the loop in the ISO 9000 quality system. Here we shall explore the standard's guidelines for:

- Using appropriate process controls to prevent nonconforming output from reaching customers
- Conveying output to customers with appropriate safeguards
- Channeling information on nonconformances into corrective actions and process improvement

Obviously, not all the requirements in these sections apply to all facilities. A maker of toothpicks, for example, may not need to implement in-depth "product identification and traceability" measures.

But at some level, the other provisions apply across the board. After all, the two most critical purposes of a quality system are

- To ensure that only verified conforming output reaches customers
- To transform causes of nonconformances into corrective actions that result in continuous improvement

These are the purposes specifically addressed by the ISO requirements.

The various parts of ISO 9000 describe quality system requirements for controlling and improving output in several different sections, as discussed in detail below:

Product Identification and Traceability

Control of Nonconforming Product

Handling, Storage, Packaging, and Delivery

Corrective Action

Product Identification and Traceability: ISO 9001, 4.8

Checklist of Requirements

- To the extent deemed appropriate to meet legal, regulatory, or quality requirements, facility should operate a documented system for identifying and tracing output throughout and/or beyond the process.

This section refers to three general types of identification and traceability systems which a facility may use.

1. Means of tracking *input* (supplied products or services) from source all the way through the process. For example, a printer may want to be able to identify the specific source of paper used for various printing projects.

2. Means of identifying specific *operations* upon the output. Operations can apply to equipment or personnel. For example, the printing facility may want to be able to trace output back to a particular press or employee.

3. Means of identifying the *ultimate destination* of output. For example, the printing facility may wish to trace the whereabouts of sensitive or important printed products, such as blank checks and stock certificates.

The extent to which a facility implements identification and traceability procedures depends upon the facility's quality needs. That is why the standard uses the term "appropriate." In some cases, these procedures may be wholly unnecessary. In other cases, they may be mandatory—required by law. Often, the need falls somewhere in between.

- Input traceability may be integral to the facility's subcontractor management system. For example, the printing facility's procedure for tracking the source of paper may be part of its ongoing evaluation of paper suppliers.

- Operational traceability may be part of procedures to monitor employee effectiveness, equipment maintenance, or other critical process-oriented characteristics.

- Traceability to destination may be a key to ensuring long-term customer satisfaction. The most obvious example of this is automobile manufacturing: automakers routinely issue recalls when problems related to safety and/or quality arise.

When identification and traceability systems are used, the standard requires that the output traced thereby be given unique identification numbers and that all such identifications be recorded.

Control of Nonconforming Product: ISO 9001, 4.13; ISO 9004, 14

Checklist of Requirements
- Facility must maintain documented procedures for the responsible segregation and disposition of nonconforming material in order to prevent its inadvertent use.

The standard's guidelines for verifying conformance to requirements were discussed in Chap. 10. These verifications can have a process-control or product orientation. They can occur at many different points in the process:

At the input phase

At various within-process phases

At the output phase

Upon delivery to the customer

Inevitably, regardless of nature, these measures will result in the identification of nonconforming material of some type. The standard makes it clear that the quality system should include procedures for controlling nonconforming product to prevent it from "inadvertent use"—that is, from reaching customers. These procedures, according to the standard, should kick in as soon as the nonconformity is detected.

ISO 9000 outlines these guidelines for controlling nonconforming product:

Responsibility. As with all other aspects of the quality system, responsibility for controlling product must be defined.

Identification. Nonconforming material should be appropriately identified. Where pertinent, other output within proximity of the nonconforming output should be examined.

Documentation. The occurrence of nonconformance should be documented at once.

Segregation. Where possible, nonconforming output should be physically segregated until disposition is made.

Evaluation. Designated and competent personnel should examine product to determine the optimal disposition.

Disposition. Output should be disposed of in accordance with documented procedures. The standard suggests four possible outcomes for nonconforming product:

- Rework (to meet specified requirements), with reinspection
- Rework for different purpose (to other specified requirements), with reinspection
- Accept with or without repair, with advice to and approval by the customer and with a record of each occurrence maintained
- Scrap

Prevention. Steps should be taken to prevent recurrence of the nonconformity. These steps may be part of an overall Corrective Action process, as described below.

Handling, Storage, Packaging, and Delivery: ISO 9001, 4.15

Checklist of Requirements

- Facility must operate a planned, controlled, and documented system to ensure that the quality integrity of materials and output is maintained up to the time of being put into use.

As noted throughout this book, the ISO quality system is comprehensive. Other quality tools and techniques cover specific aspects of output design and production. ISO 9000 is a structured cycle of activities—beginning and ending with the customer—that governs the quality of output from conception to final delivery.

ISO 9000, then, asserts that quality measures must be extensive enough to ensure the quality integrity of output not only to the end of the production process but also, if appropriate, to the point where the customer has put the output into use.

This section of the standard explains the elements of the quality system that are intended to ensure quality through the delivery or installation stage. The standard refers to these elements as part of a "documented system" for the "proper planning and control" of materials and output. The following factors are taken into account:

- *Identification* of all materials and output should be made in accordance with procedures and specifications.

- *Packaging* should be appropriate to use and environment, consistent with the contract, and governed by written procedures.

- *Handling and storage* should be appropriate to the protection of the output and its shelf life, and consistent with the contract. The facility should have procedures for periodic inspection of stored items.

- *Delivery* should be conducted in accordance with procedures aimed at protecting the quality of product.

- *Installation* should, once again, be covered by documented procedures. These should provide for necessary instructional documents or other measures aimed at minimizing improper installation or use. Warnings as to hazards and safety should also be clearly documented.

Corrective Action: ISO 9001, 4.14; ISO 9004, 14, 15

Checklist of Requirements

- Responsibility for handling nonconformity and corrective action should be defined and documented.

- Nonconforming material should be identified and segregated until disposition.

- Nonconforming material should be reviewed and disposed of in accordance with defined procedures.

- Nonconformances should be evaluated to assess their impact on overall quality and customer satisfaction.

- Causes of nonconformances should be identified, and appropriate corrective actions designed and implemented.

- Where appropriate, permanent process changes should be implemented to prevent the recurrence of systemic nonconformances.

- Handling of nonconformity and correction action activities should be documented in accordance with procedures.

By now, you can discern the cycle or system created by ISO 9000's requirements. The quality system verifies conformance to requirements and makes the conformance status visible. Output which conforms goes on to the next step.

This section addresses the standard's guidelines for handling nonconforming output. These are, arguably, the most important sections of ISO 9000. The guidelines here are intended to ensure that (1) nonconforming output is prevented from reaching customers and (2) causes of nonconformance are identified and corrected ("continuous improvement").

The quality system should be structured to mesh the processing of nonconformity with corrective action. This is the best way to ensure consistent and continuous improvement of quality at all levels.

The guidelines of the standard can be expressed in the following steps:

Responsibility. As is true with every other aspect of the quality system, responsibility for handling nonconformance and taking corrective action should be assigned and documented. A specific coordinating activity for corrective action should be specified.

Identification. Obviously, all nonconformities must be identified—usually as a function of the verification activities described above.

Segregation. When possible, nonconforming material should be segregated from conforming material to prevent it from being released inadvertently and to ensure its proper disposition.

Disposition. Possibilities here include:

- Reworking material to render it conforming.
- Obtaining approval from the next process step to accept as is. Usually some concession will be required from the customer. Such activity should be thoroughly documented.
- Reclassifying material to a different grade or category in which it conforms to prevailing requirements.
- Disposal.

Evaluation. The nonconformance should be studied to assess its impact on costs, performance, and customer satisfaction, and to determine the facility's level of response in terms of corrective action.

Investigation. Processes, operations, records, customer complaints, and the like should be carried out to determine the root cause of the nonconformance.

Preventive action. The facility should respond with a corrective action that is appropriate to the existing and potential impact of the nonconformance on quality and customer satisfaction. Preventive actions may entail any or all of the following:

- Process changes
- Specification changes
- Quality system changes

Process controls. Implementation of corrective action should be coupled with process controls sufficient to ensure the efficacy of the corrections and to facilitate later review and necessary adjustment. Process controls may be temporary or permanent, as appropriate.

Documentation. As with all other essential elements of the quality system, handling of nonconformances and development and implementation of corrective actions should be appropriately documented.

ISO 9000 cautions that preventive and corrective actions must be more than just effective against the specific problems. They must also be proportional to the magnitude of the problem and not inimical to associated processes.

PART 3

Putting ISO 9000 to Work

12

Implementing ISO 9000

*Thing about Americans is, we're always
looking for the catch. We're always trying
to figure out the easiest and least painful
way to get something done. Usually this
means paying someone to do the dirty work
for us. But you can't do that with ISO.
Because it's your system. It's about your
facility, your products, your ways of doing
things. You can't hire a consultant to plug
ISO in for you. A consultant can guide
you, but that's all. You have to do the rest.*

ANTHONY COGGESHALL
Adhesives Research, Inc.
Registered to ISO 9001

Suppose you want to put ISO 9000 to work in your facility. Perhaps
you have a shot at a major new account, but ISO 9000 certification is
required before the client will even talk to you. ("Don't even bother
with a proposal until you're certified.")

Maybe your biggest customer has told you that your main competitor has become ISO 9000 certified. ("People over there claim it's improved quality 300 percent. What do you think?")

Or—even more traumatic—your primary customer is requiring ISO 9000 certification of its entire supplier network. ("We're cutting our supplier group by half. Anybody not ISO certified is out.")

Or maybe your facility has no formal quality system now, but management has decided that a quality system is a key to maintaining and expanding markets.

Implementing an ISO 9000 quality system is no different from making any other major, fundamental, far-reaching change in your organization. Like the old joke about mating elephants, it comes with much roaring and screaming—and it can take two years to see the results.

In plain terms, how difficult is implementing ISO 9000? The answer depends on many factors. The amount of pain, expense, and time required to implement ISO 9000 depends upon

- The sophistication of your existing quality program
- The size of your facility
- The complexity of your process

Implementing an ISO 9000 quality system is, in fact, as simple as

- Knowing the requirements of the standard
- Understanding the facility and its processes
- Committing the resources
- Planning well
- Seeing it through

Add to both of these lists one other factor, the biggest one, the grandparent of them all: management commitment. Without that, all else is for naught. "Top management needs to know a lot about ISO 9000," says Jim Ecklein of Augustine Medical. "We gave our managers a lot of training in it, got them walking, talking, breathing ISO."

If you are a career quality professional, all of this probably sounds very familiar to you. No surprise. In terms of implementation, ISO 9000 is not much different from any other quality tool or technique. Same tough sell. Same painful transition period. Same frustrations. Same profound impact.

Implementation of ISO 9000 differs from that of other quality programs in that it affects the entire organization. When faithfully and aggressively pursued, it results in that always coveted, seldom realized "cultural transition" to an atmosphere of continuous improvement. There are other advantages, too. Things like:

- Improved customer satisfaction
- Increased competitive strength
- Greater market share

and all those other benefits described in Chap. 3.

But it is virtually impossible to get there until you undergo a formal ISO 9000 implementation cycle. Take the word of one who tried. "We wrote an ISO 9000 quality manual," says Don Van Hook of Strahman Valves, "but the consultant who came in and assessed it said it needed work; no way would we be approved." With the help of the consultant, Strahman is well along in a formal ISO 9000 implementation program.

In fact, according to a report in *Compliance Engineering,* 70 percent of all companies that "do not pursue preassessment or preparation services" (i.e., implementation) fail the ISO 9000 "preassessment the first time through."

This chapter examines the steps of ISO 9000 implementation. Some of the observations here are broad enough to apply to quality improvement programs in general. Others are specific to ISO 9000. The main focus is on creating an implementation process which (1) gets an ISO 9000 quality system up and running and (2) if desired, prepares the facility to apply for formal ISO 9000 registration. The registration process is the subject of Chap. 13.

The Absolute Prerequisite: Top Management Commitment

Deming said it. Juran said it. Crosby, Feigenbaum, Peters said it. Every quality consultant says it and most company managers concur. Without it no quality initiative can succeed; with it no quality initiative—including ISO 9000 implementation—can fail.

That is how important top management commitment is.

Ireland's Lorcan Mooney, ISO 9000 consultant, implementor, and quality systems assessor, says: "The most significant pitfall in ISO implementation is the CEO being uncommitted, or opting out, or standing on the sidelines and expecting other people to do it."

Management Responsibility guidelines come first in the standard because its creators understood that without management involvement and participation, nothing fruitful can happen.

So it is with ISO 9000 implementation. In this context, commitment is much more than approving purchase orders and observing pep rallies. The CEO cannot delegate commitment and passion and resolve. The CEO cannot remain passive, let alone skeptical, and expect to see results. It is said that 80 percent of success is showing up. With ISO 9000 implementation, the figure is more like 100 percent. Top management must show up.

What is more, top management has to be an active, daily, visible presence in the process. Brian Burke of Container Products Corp. observes: "Top management people have to understand and do more than just accept the tenets of the ISO 9000 process. They have to lead it. They don't necessarily have to get involved in the nitty-gritty, but they have to lead and drive and apply pressure when necessary."

Where does this type of top management/CEO commitment come from? In facilities implementing ISO 9000 today, there seem to be several sources:

- Direct marketplace pressure: requirements of crucial customers or parent conglomerates
- Indirect marketplace pressure: increased quality levels and visibility among competitors
- Growth ambitions: desire to exploit EC market opportunities
- Personal belief in the value of quality as a goal and quality systems as a means of reaching that goal

One of these forces is usually enough to inspire top management interest in ISO 9000. True commitment usually springs from some combination of the above. It is not something that can be imposed 100 percent upon the CEO. Much of it has to come from genuine conviction.

But once top management commitment is there, CEOs make ISO 9000 implementation, and operation of the quality system, a top corporate priority—and make sure that managers never forget it. This is certainly the case at Container Products, where, according to Brian Burke:

> The CEO chairs quarterly meetings of our top plant managers. At each meeting, plant managers present various reports on key business areas: financial, operations, and sales. Usually, since our CEO is a finance type, the first items reported upon are the financials. When we started implementing ISO 9002, I suggested to the CEO that he have managers present status reports on ISO 9002 implementation first, even before the financials. That's what he did. It caught the plant managers off guard—but it spoke loud and clear as to the priorities of the organization.

A quality professional whose firm has become registered to ISO 9000 relates another example of CEO firmness:

> One of the VPs walked into his office and told the CEO that ISO 9000 was never going to work here, and that he didn't want to be involved. The president's answer was "Either sign on or you're out of here." Needless to say, the VP signed on. So did everyone else.

Contrast that with the experience of another quality professional, struggling to implement ISO 9000 in an automotive manufacturing plant in the northeast:

> You've *got* to have management commitment behind you. When we started out, our managers told me they were committed, but now I know they aren't. How did I find out? When I called some meetings to discuss ISO—and no one showed up.

One would charitably have to call that ISO 9000 implementation program an uphill battle.

Establish Implementation Teams

ISO 9000 is implemented not by magic, but by people. The first phase of implementation calls for the commitment of top management—the CEO and perhaps a handful of other key people. The next step is to create a personnel structure to plan and oversee implementation.

The first component of this personnel structure—and the most important one, after the CEO—is the *management representative* (MR). In the context of the standard, the MR is the person within the facility who acts as interface between facility management and the ISO 9000 registrar.

But the role is really much broader than that. The MR should also act as the facility's "quality system champion," the protector of the vision. The MR must be a person with:

- Access to and total backing of the CEO
- Genuine and passionate commitment to quality in general and the ISO 9000 quality system in particular
- The clout—resulting from rank, seniority, or both—to influence managers and others of all levels and functions
- Detailed knowledge of quality methods in general and ISO 9000 in particular

In a perfect world, the CEO would act as the management representative. In the real world, this is almost always impractical. But the MR should be a person who enjoys the trust, confidence, and total backing of the CEO. He or she should also have the respect of other employees at the facility.

Next, a top-level implementation team is created. In some firms this is called the Quality Action Council. In others it is known as the Quality Steering Committee. The team is usually chaired by the MR and consists of:

The CEO

Top managers

Key functional managers

Top union representative (if applicable)

The Quality Action Council is mainly a policy group. It sets objectives for quality system implementation, approves plans, evaluates reports, and prescribes changes as needed. The council also makes critical decisions about the quality system documentation. Its members should decide early on who (1) is responsible for writing, editing, and approving the facility's quality manual and (2) who is responsible for second-tier and (if utilized) third-tier documentation.

Next comes a network of Quality Action Teams. In small to midsize facilities, these teams are organized by department or function. Each is headed by the functional manager or department head, who in turn sits on the Quality Action Council. Larger facilities have more elaborate action networks, but the objective is the same: to have a team of line people representing each critical facility function and process element. Whatever organization is devised, there must be a clear and visible reporting and communication network all the way up to the MR and the Quality Action Council.

All members of the Quality Action Teams are knowledgeable about the process elements in which they work. That is the main criterion for membership. It is helpful, though not required, that they also have some advanced familiarity with ISO 9000 quality systems. But familiarity can be provided by an ensuing training cycle.

The Quality Action Teams are the hands-on element of the ISO 9000 implementation effort. They execute the policy devised by the council. They make the quality system happen.

There is one other "people" issue: Should facilities engage the services of an outside consultant? Most find that this step pays major dividends in reducing implementation time and expense and increasing effectiveness. Larger organizations with multiple facilities to implement often employ a full-time specialist to help them get their ISO 9000 quality systems up and running.

Assess Current Quality System Status

As we have seen in our review of the ISO 9000 technical requirements, there is little new or novel about the quality system. Most of its elements are a combination of good common sense as well as "the best of" quality methods, techniques, and philosophies that have been around for years.

Keep this in mind as you begin the implementation process. There is nothing in the ISO 9000 standard that requires duplication of effort, redundant systems, or make-work. On the contrary: the goal of ISO 9000 is to create a quality system that conforms to the standard. This does not preclude incorporating, adapting, and adding onto quality programs already in place. In fact, the standard encourages facilities to do just that.

So the next step in the implementation process is to compare the facility's existing quality programs—and quality system, if there is one—with the requirements of the standard. Program assessment can be done internally, if the knowledge level is there. Or a formal preassessment can be obtained from any one of a large number of ISO 9000 consulting, implementing, and registration firms.

Facilities which are already subject to customer quality audits often find that their existing system meets a sizable number of the ISO requirements. This is especially true of facilities conforming to the various military standards. Dennis Beckley of Dayton-Rogers found that MIL STD 45208 and 45662 had many elements found in ISO. David Turtletaub of Phillips Circuit Assembly, which conforms to MIL-Q-9858, says that standard "is parallel to ISO in many ways. The intent is the same except for two or three different areas. They share many of the section titles, groupings, and wording of the various subsections."

The same is true for other customer-mandated quality standards such as General Motors' Targets for Excellence. Says George Raub of TRW: "If you interpret it broadly, TFE has everything that ISO has. It's not as explicit in its documentation requirements and does not require the quality that ISO has. Also, TFE does not require quality manual approval."

Facilities which have subscribed to Malcolm Baldrige National Quality Award criteria also find their ISO 9000 implementation path easier than others. "GE Automation," according to *Managing Automation* magazine, "had an easier time than many in winning ISO 9001 registration . . . because the company had previously applied for the Malcolm Baldrige National Quality Award. It already had extensive outside comment on its quality procedures."

Facilities with formal quality systems already in place are well on their way toward implementing full-fledged ISO 9000 quality systems. For those without quality systems, implementation can be quite an uphill battle. Sandy Weller of Woodbridge Foam Corporation is responsible for implementing an ISO 9002 quality system in a facility which has had no quality systems at all. Her assessment? "It's no fun."

Ideally, the assessment is conducted at several levels. The Quality Action Council focuses on the larger elements of the ISO 9000 standard—including Management Responsibility, Quality System, Quality Costs, Quality Audits, and Personnel and Training. (See Chap. 5.) Quality Action Teams compare the standard's requirements with systems and procedures in their own functional areas. The main purpose of these assessments is to get a clear picture of the state of the facility's quality program as it compares with the ISO 9000 standard. The teams should pinpoint systems which conform, systems which can be adapted, and, most critically, areas of nonconformance.

As with so many other aspects of ISO 9000 implementation, the assessment process can often be beneficial on its own merits. At Adhesives Research, department members assessed one another. "That gave all of us a chance to vent our venom," says Anthony Coggeshall. "It didn't hurt the process—it actually helped it: because we got all that good and bad and peripheral garbage out on table, where we could sort through it and fix it up and prioritize it."

Information gathered in the self-assessment should be documented and channeled to the Quality Action Council. If the assessment is conducted with the help of an outside body, that organization will usually provide specific implementation direction at the same time.

Create a Documented Implementation Plan

Once the facility has obtained a clear picture of how its quality system compares with the ISO 9000 standard, all nonconformances must be addressed with a documented implementation plan.

This plan may be created by an ad hoc committee under the authority of the Quality Action Council. Usually, the plan calls for setting up procedures to make the facility's quality system fully compliant with the standard. Procedures which affect high-level policy elements of the quality system may be handled by the council itself, or by designated members. Others may be handed down to various Quality Action Teams for development.

The implementation plan should be thorough and specific, detailing:

- Procedures to be developed
- Objective of the system
- Pertinent ISO 9000 section
- Person or team responsible
- Approval required
- Training required
- Resources required
- Estimated completion date

These elements should be organized into a detailed GANTT chart, to be reviewed and approved by the Quality Action Council. Once approved, the plan and its GANTT chart should be controlled by the MR. The chart should be reviewed and updated at each council meeting as the implementation process proceeds.

As mentioned earlier, areas requiring implementation can vary widely from facility to facility, and depend upon the type and level of quality system elements already in place. Some facilities, with long-standing total quality management (TQM) or other quality systems, may need only rudimentary implementation measures in order to deal with nonconformances. Others may require the development of full-blown quality systems—a process which can take months, if not years.

Most facilities with some level of quality program already in place find that their biggest areas of nonconformance are in

Design (for ISO 9001)

Purchasing

Inspection and testing

Process control

Dennis Beckley of Dayton-Rogers found that management responsibility was a weak area in the quality system. "We have had good management commitment," he says. "We've been operating a TQM program for four years. We have mission statements and so forth, but management responsibility was not an area addressed in our manual or quality system per se."

Another potential problem area is training. Most facilities have training programs of some sort, and many programs are in fact very good. Where they sometimes fall short of ISO requirements is in the needs-assessment area. "Our training program was basically reactive," notes Brian Burke of Container Products. "When training was necessary, we did it. We didn't follow ISO's proactive approach—constantly evaluating training needs to see what we should be doing."

Among American firms, the area most notorious for nonconformance is *documentation*. More on this below.

Provide Training

Obviously, the implementation plan will have provided for training in various functional areas of the quality system being implemented. Certain training needs will depend on the nonconformances being addressed. The Quality Action Teams should take responsibility for providing specific training in their respective functional areas.

In addition, more general training needs are attendant to implementation and apply to virtually all facilities. Since the ISO 9000 quality system affects all areas and all personnel in the organization, it is wise to provide basic orientation in the quality system standard to all employees. This can be a one-day program which educates personnel about quality systems in general and the ISO 9000 quality system in particular.

Adhesives Research had just such a formal program. "We set up a formal ISO 9000 training syllabus for management, supervisory, and hourly people," says Anthony Coggeshall. "It was not lengthy, just a good overview, supported by transparencies, covering basically what ISO 9000 was and, more importantly, what it was not."

The training program should emphasize the benefits that the facility expects to realize through its ISO 9000 quality system. The program should also stress the higher levels of participation and self-direction that the quality system renders to employees. Such a focus will go far to enlist employee support and commitment.

"We had no problem getting our hourly people on board," says Sandy Weller of Woodbridge Foam Corp. "They were really happy that they were getting some say. That seems to have been the big thing, that our people were getting some say."

David Turtletaub of Phillips Circuit Assembly agrees. "Our people were very favorable. They liked to see the structure being implemented to help them out in their jobs. They also liked the uniform approach to the different areas of the facility. And it helped for them to know that the facility management group was solidly behind the program—from the president and the general manager level on down."

Finally, the Quality Action Council should create and distribute a standard for procedure writing at the facility. This step will ensure that all procedures—the heart of the quality system's documentation—are consistent and relevant.

Create Documentation

As noted earlier, documentation is the most common area of nonconformance among American facilities wishing to implement ISO 9000 quality systems. As Don Van Hook of Strahman Valves observes: "When we started our implementation, we found that documentation was inadequate. Even absent, in some areas. Take calibration. Obviously it's necessary, and obviously we do it, but it wasn't being documented. Another area was inspection and testing. We inspect and test practically every item that leaves here, but our documentation was inadequate."

There is no way around it: documentation is mandatory. It is essential to the ISO 9000 registration process because it provides objective evidence of the status of the quality system.

The two basic rules of ISO documentation are:

Document what you do.

Do what you document.

Many facilities find that their existing documentation is adequate in most respects. To bring it into full ISO conformance, they implement control procedures to ensure that documentation is available as needed and is reviewed, updated, stored, and disposed of in a planned, orderly manner.

In this context, documentation refers mainly to procedures. Under the ISO 9000 quality system, all work which affects quality must be planned, controlled, and documented. In other words, people whose work affects quality should know how to do that work in a way that maximizes quality. Toward that end, detailed written procedures and work instructions must be created where, as the standard states, the absence of same would adversely affect quality.

For many facilities, the process can become nightmarish. Don Van Hook observes: "One of hardest things to do is to get shop people to become what they think of as bookkeepers. They don't like paperwork. To many of them it's a dirty word."

But the process of creating and using documentation is central to the effectiveness of quality system implementation. For one thing, the exercise is almost always educational. Many facilities that find the creation of work procedures and instructions to be a difficult process are facilities that have never had such things before. Typically, important process work—even work with a serious impact on quality—is done in an unplanned, inconsistent manner.

Quality system documentation forces the facility, at all levels, to think through exactly what is being done and how it is being done. Most firms find this to be a positive learning experience.

- It disseminates knowledge of the process.

- It pools process knowledge and expertise.

- It creates positive interfaces among individuals and process elements.

Through these interfaces, people develop positive, proactive approaches to teamwork and quality.

- They learn how to work together better.

- They learn what to expect of one another.

- They establish communication channels that result in positive improvement.

This is far more powerful, and far more important, than the mere process of writing down procedures and work instructions. But writing them down is a vital part of the documentation process, too. Written documentation is

- Evidence that thought has been given to the procedures
- An irreplaceable reference resource for outside assessors
- An invaluable training and improvement tool

Keep in mind that quality system documentation does not need to be exhaustive, exhausting, or redundant. It is certainly not intended to be an end in itself. Again, ISO 9000 requires only that the facility have documentation—procedures, work instructions, and the like—where the absence of same would adversely affect quality. The facility must maintain the minimal amount of documentation necessary to demonstrate that its quality systems exist and are being operated.

As you have probably gathered, the process of creating the needed documentation can be arduous. And there is one major pitfall to be avoided: make sure that procedures and work instructions are created by the people who actually do the work.

Sandy Weller of Woodbridge Foam says that her facility went about the task another way: "At first, I wrote the procedures, not the people doing the work. So when we put the procedures into practice, the people doing the work had some problems. But we're working out the bugs."

Dennis Beckley of Dayton-Rogers had a similar experience. He and other corporate implementors played a major role in creating quality documentation and manuals for the various facilities implementing ISO 9000. "We tailored the documentation to one plant's way of doing things. At our corporate quality meetings, plant managers reviewed the documentation and approved it. Then we audited the plants and found out they were doing things their own way and not following the procedures. From a corporate standpoint, it can be tough to get everyone to do what's in the documentation."

Even though procedures and instructions should be documented by the people actually doing the work, associated middle managers should be involved in the process, too. The experience of Container Products demonstrates how important this involvement is. According to Brian Burke, in most of Container Products plants the quality assurance people worked directly with the line people on the procedures. "Even though the supervisors and product managers signed off on the procedures, they were not nearly as enthusiastic about implementing them as were the supervisors in the plant, where everyone was included in the process."

The final link in the documentation chain is the facility's *quality manual*. The contents of the manual were examined in detail in Chap. 6. From an implementation standpoint, creation of the quality manual is driven by the top-level Quality Action Council, which draws upon the systems, procedures, and documentation created and implemented by the Quality Action Teams. The quality manual must address, point by point, the components of the ISO 9000 quality system being implemented. Ultimately, the quality manual is

- The blueprint for the facility's quality system
- The cross-reference of the facility's quality procedures
- The expression of the facility's quality commitment

Document Control

Once the necessary quality system documentation has been generated, a documented system must be created for controlling it. As noted in the Technical Requirements and Guidelines sections, control is simply a means of managing the creation, approval, distribution, revision, storage, and disposal of the various types of documentation. Document control systems should be as simple and as easy to operate as possible—sufficient to meet ISO requirements and that is all.

The principle of ISO 9000 document control is that employees should have access to the documentation and records needed to fulfill their responsibilities. Ironically, direct access can often result in certain employees having *less* recordkeeping and documentation to deal with—and can be a cause of resistance. The facility's quality manual is a primary example. "We got minor resistance from some major players who were used to having the quality manual, but who didn't really need to have their own copy if it," says Jim Ecklein of Augustine Medical. "We solved that by having a master quality manual, with references to submanuals for each facility area. That way, people had what they needed, but we weren't passing quality manuals out to people who didn't really need it and wouldn't use it."

Monitor Progress

When the procedures have been completed and the quality system fleshed out, it is time to put the quality system into effect. In this extremely important phase, management must pay close attention to results to make sure that the elements of the quality system are logical and effective.

Effective monitoring is what makes or breaks ISO 9000 implementation. It is also the ultimate measure of how well—or poorly—facility management is living up to its responsibilities, as described in the Management Responsibility section of the standard. Says ISO consultant Lorcan Mooney, "A serious threat to effective ISO 9000 implementation is failure to monitor development as the process proceeds."

In particular, management at all levels should keep an eye out for

- Gaps and assumptions in procedures
- Steps which are difficult, ineffective, or impractical

Many such problems can be dealt with by the Quality Action Teams. Resulting changes should, of course, be documented and approved in accordance with procedures provided for in the quality system.

Management, up to the level of the Quality Action Council, should simultaneously carry out its review functions as prescribed by the standard and by its own documented procedures. These activities include

Internal audits

Formal corrective actions

Management reviews

It is especially helpful to begin the internal audit program immediately as part of implementation, thereby solving many implementation problems at the "local" level. "We have internal audits every four weeks," says Anthony Coggeshall of Adhesives Research. "Each team consists of members of two unrelated departments—not the quality department, and not the department being audited. These audits are really forums for departments to talk to one another and solve their own problems."

Dennis Beckley's organization, Dayton-Rogers, follows a similar practice but on a multiple-facility basis. "We have ISO champions in each plant, and each is going to our other plants to conduct internal audits in accordance with the internal audit plan we created. This includes corrective action and follow-up as needed."

Inevitably, it will become evident that certain individuals in the facility are unenthusiastic about the effective implementation of the quality system. (Outright resistance or obstruction is, of course, a disciplinary matter beyond the scope of this book.) How should management handle reluctant participants? Should it make a special effort to win them over?

No, says Lorcan Mooney. "Focus your efforts on the people who are already sold on ISO," he advises. "Don't concentrate on winning over the lukewarm or the uncommitted. Give it time. Sometimes, peer pressure—seeing coworkers thrive under the system—does the trick. In other cases, the quality system itself does the convincing. When you get a few wins under your belt, a lot of those people will fall off the fence on your side."

Review: Pitfalls to Effective Implementation

Here is a brief checklist of the most significant barriers to effective ISO 9000 quality system implementation.

1. *Lack of CEO commitment.* As Lorcan Mooney says, "If senior management consists of four or five people, and two of them are not committed, over time they can be won over. But if the CEO is not committed, then in no way are you going to win in the long run."

2. *Failure to involve everyone in the process.* Ownership and empowerment are key to effective implementation. To help employees feel

like owners of their activity, make them responsible for developing and documenting their procedures.

3. *Failure to monitor progress and enforce deadlines.*

Notice that all three of these pitfalls are directly traceable to management—or lack of it.

Outcomes: Positive

When effectively implemented, ISO 9000 quality systems provide positive benefits almost at once. "Of course we started with nothing," says Sandy Weller of Woodbridge Foam. "But almost from the start we noticed a major reduction in errors. Just the process of putting in the system, documenting what we were doing, and keeping track of what was going on improved quality—because it made everyone aware of his or her impact on quality."

13
Registering to ISO 9000

We have been well pleased with the registration process. The registrar we're dealing with has strong ethical standards and shares our philosophies and goals about quality.

BRIAN BURKE
Container Products Co.
ISO 9002 Candidate

A facility registers to ISO 9000, or becomes certified (the terms are interchangeable), in order to obtain objective third-party verification that its quality system conforms to the ISO 9000 standard.

The facility may undergo the registration process simply to reinforce its own quality program and commitment. There are other reasons as well. Some facilities register:

- As a proactive step to counter competition and secure new business, especially in the European Community
- In response to a competitive threat
- In response to customer requirements
- In response to the requirements of a parent organization, as is often the case among multinationals

Finally, some firms—very few at this point, but the number may grow—register because they are obliged to by legal and/or regulatory authority.

The registration process itself is rather simple. Compared with creating and implementing an ISO 9000 quality system, registration may seem almost anticlimactic. Most American facilities today find that the biggest problem with registration is getting past the obstacles, confusion, and misinformation that are rife in the marketplace.

This chapter explores the ISO 9000 registration process in detail. It attempts to clear away the obstacles, sort out the confusion, and replace bad information with good. Currently the situation with respect to recruiting registrars, gaining accreditation, and other matters is in a high state of flux. The information presented here is considered to be accurate as of press time. But for the best help, prudent managers will seek the counsel of recognized ISO 9000 practitioners.

As indicated in earlier chapters, some facilities rush into the process of applying for ISO 9000 registration before they are ready. This explains why some 70 percent of initial ISO 9000 registration applications fail on the first go-around.

Before applying for ISO 9000 registration, it is imperative that your facility has:

- Implemented a quality system that meets the technical requirements of the part of the ISO 9000 quality system standard to which you seek registration (ISO 9001, 9002, or 9003)
- Documented it with a quality manual and subordinate procedures, work instructions, and other materials
- Operated it successfully for three, and preferably six, months

These are the preparatory steps which have been detailed earlier in this book. Once they are accomplished, the typical facility takes the following additional steps to obtain ISO 9000 registration:

- Establish a relationship with an ISO 9000 registrar whose scope of accreditation covers the facility's field of activity
- File a formal application
- Undergo an assessment of documentation

- Undergo an on-site assessment of the quality system

- Remedy nonconformances by completing any required corrective action requests

- Pay the associated fees

    The first step is, by far, the trickiest.

Engaging an ISO 9000 Registrar

There are in excess of 40 registration firms operating in the United States today. Some bear very familiar names, such as Underwriters Laboratories. Other names, such as Det Norske Veritas, are less familiar. How does a facility go about recruiting an ISO 9000 registrar? Very carefully.

Finding a registrar is not at all tough. It is as easy as looking in the Yellow Pages. But, especially in the United States, registrars are not created equal. All can provide some sort of "registration." But not all can give you the type of registration that will help you meet your goals.

Why so? The short answer: The United States does not have a government-sanctioned accreditation body. To understand what this means, let us take a look at the European sphere for a moment.

The Registration Process Overseas

In Britain, for example, the responsibilities for ISO 9000 are well defined, understood, and recognized.

- The top-level authority involved in quality systems registration (to BS 5750 and ISO 9000) is the British government's Department of Trade and Industry (DT&I).

- Since 1985, DT&I has sponsored the National Accreditation Council for Certifying Bodies (NACCB). This organization accredits—in effect, provides a stamp of approval on—quality system registrars.

- These registrars conform to the requirements of the NACCB and are authorized to issue a registration stamp bearing the NACCB logo.

- Each registrar is accredited to provide quality system registration in certain specified vertical markets. The range of markets that registrars operate in is referred to collectively as their "scope."

(See Fig. 13-1.)

So, if you are a British facility which makes concrete pipe, finding a registrar is relatively simple. Various publications list the NACCB-accredited registrars; you simply look up a registrar whose scope includes concrete pipe, make a call, and go from there.

Most EC nations have accreditation bodies equivalent to NACCB. These bodies, which conform to requirements published by the EC's European Committee for Quality System Assessment and Certification (CQS), include the RvC of the Netherlands. Some extend reciprocal recognition to other accrediting bodies; some do not.

There is a separate training and accreditation channel which applies to ISO 9000 assessors. ISO publishes qualifications criteria for quality systems assessors in ISO 10011. The Registration Board for Assessors (RBA) in Britain is the body empowered to sanction and approve assessor training and certification schemes. RBA is the only

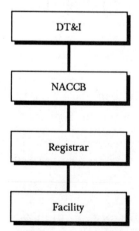

Figure 13-1. Registration hierarchy in the United Kingdom.

body of its type at this time; plans are afoot to create similar assessor training and certification bodies in other EC countries.

What this bureaucratic Byzantium amounts to is that a firm wishing to obtain ISO 9000 registration which is recognized and accepted in the EC should deal with a registrar that

- Is accredited by the NACCB or an equivalent body
- Uses assessors whose credentials are traceable to RBA

Registration for U.S. Facilities

As if that isn't confusing enough, the situation gets even murkier for U.S. facilities.

Suppose your facility is a concrete pipe maker located in the United States. You are seeking ISO 9000 registration to help you meet requirements of customers in the EC. When you set out in search of a registrar for help, you discover that there are no U.S. equivalents to NACCB or RBA—no agencies approved by the American government to accredit registrars or assessors.

The U.S. government does express an interest in and commitment to quality improvement. It operates the tiny Federal Quality Institute (Office of Personnel Management/Office of Management and Budget), sponsors the Malcolm Baldrige National Quality Award (Department of Commerce), and promotes total quality management in its various agencies, including the Defense Department and its suppliers.

But unlike Britain and other EC nations, the U.S. government has not endorsed an ISO 9000 or equivalent quality system standard. It does not sponsor an accrediting body such as NACCB or RBA. It does not provide recognition of or support to domestic registrars. Essentially, any organization in the United States can identify itself as a "quality system registrar" and issue ISO 9000 registration stamps, even if its only authority is granted by itself.

In fact, there is at present a widely publicized American equivalent to ISO 9000. Known as ASQC/ANSI Q90, this standard is sponsored by the American Society for Quality Control, a private industry trade group with no U.S. government approval or backing. In a joint venture with the American National Standards Institute (ANSI), the

American representative to ISO, ASQC publishes a word-for-word equivalent of the ISO 9000–9004 series. It also operates a subsidiary known as the Registrar Accreditation Board (RAB), which has, on its own initiative, accredited a group of private American firms to be Q90 registrars.

It is important for U.S. facilities to understand that RAB's authority to accredit registrars is self-generated. Unlike NACCB, which operates under the aegis of a department of the British government, RAB has no U.S. government relationship or sanction. EC member nations, accrediting bodies, registrars, and firms are under no obligation to recognize or honor ISO 9000 "registrations" granted by RAB or by any other registrar whose authority is not traceable to NACCB or an EC-sanctioned equivalent.

So, though registrations issued by RAB-accredited registrars may be worthwhile for their own sake, they may not carry the same weight in the EC as registrations granted by NACCB-accredited registrars. Facilities with ISO 9000 registration from RAB-accredited registrars may find that they are not recognized or accepted in EC nations as valid ISO 9000 registrations.

In the years ahead, this situation will no doubt change. At some point the U.S. government may become an active sponsor of an equivalent to the ISO 9000 quality system standard. It may also, like the British government, put its official blessing on bodies empowered to accredit U.S. registrars. At that time, perhaps EC nations will recognize native U.S. registration on a reciprocal basis.

But these changes may be years away—and in order to protect and build EC markets, many U.S. facilities need ISO 9000 registration now. They run the risk of investing much time and money in ISO 9000 registration, only to discover that the registration "mark" is not accepted as valid in the EC. As *Industry Week* magazine observed in August 1991, "ISO 9000 registration in one country does not necessarily translate into recognition and acceptance in another."

So it is recommended that you study the credentials of potential ISO 9000 registrars carefully. First, make sure the registrar's scope covers facilities like yours. Then ask the registrar the following questions:

- What body accredited you to provide ISO 9000 registration? (NACCB or equivalent?)

- Is your ISO 9000 registration mark recognized and accepted throughout the EC?

- Most especially: Is your ISO 9000 registration mark recognized and accepted in the nation(s) in which we want to do business?

Fortunately, such registrars exist and can be readily located if you ask the right questions. Underwriters Laboratories, for example, has a memorandum of understanding with the British Standards Institute (BSI), which is accredited by NACCB and, perhaps, the most widely recognized registration body in Europe. Facilities that work with UL can obtain BSI's ISO 9000 registration at the same time.

The moral: know your registrar!

Preliminary Steps

The precise procedures for applying for registration vary from registrar to registrar. But the sequence of events is fairly uniform. Keep in mind that the process is greatly influenced by

Facility size

Facility scope

Extent of documentation

Participation of facility management

Conformance of quality system to the ISO standard

Smaller facilities with straightforward processes and by-the-numbers quality systems generally find the registration process to be a clean and brisk one. Larger facilities with complex operations, and those with ill-defined or poorly documented quality systems, can find the registration process to be extended and often quite difficult.

Sometimes, prior to initiating a formal application, registrars conduct a more comprehensive "preassessment" of the facility. The purpose of this preassessment is to verify that the facility has at least the essentials of an ISO 9000 quality system in place. Facilities which have not had the assistance of experienced ISO 9000 assessors and implementors would be wise to request such a preassessment as part of their ISO 9000 implementation process.

As Jim Ecklein of Augustine Medical notes: "Preassessment helps your registrar develop an understanding of your facility, process, and product. And it gives your people an idea of what assessments are like; it calms their nerves. Once you've been through a preassessment, you won't be as nervous when it's time for the formal registration audit.

"My feeling is, if you don't mind failing your first registration audit, don't bother getting a preassessment."

The Registration Application

Normally, the first step is for the facility to file a formal application with the registrar. With this application, the facility pays an application fee and, usually, completes a questionnaire about its operation. From the facility's responses, the registrar makes an initial judgment as to the facility's state of readiness for ISO 9000 registration.

Most registrars also conduct an off-site assessment of the facility's quality system documentation. This is in fact a formal review of the facility's quality manual.

If the registrar determines, through its review of the questionnaire or the quality manual, that the quality system has serious nonconformances, it so informs the facility. At that point, the registration process halts until the facility can show that it has corrected the nonconformances. Note that registrars are barred from providing guidance as to correcting nonconformances or from giving any further assistance, such as training and consulting services. The facility must obtain these from other sources.

Initial Assessment

Once the registrar has satisfied itself that the quality system depicted in the quality manual conforms to ISO 9000 standards, it schedules an on-site "audit" or "assessment" of the facility. (ISO documentation uses both terms interchangeably. Since Guide 48, the principal ISO publication on the subject, uses only "assessment," that term will be preferred in this book.)

Usually, the facility is allowed to pick the date for the initial assessment. On that date the facility should be prepared to undergo inspection of its facility, quality system, records, and other documentation by the assessment team.

The inspection team is composed of quality system assessors—credentialed, accredited, highly qualified individuals. The standards for accreditation of quality system assessors are set by bodies specially created for this purpose.

In England, for example, quality system assessors are accredited by the National Registration Scheme for Assessors of Quality Systems, under the aegis of the Department of Trade and Industry. The administering body is the Registration Board for Assessors (RBA), which is to quality system assessors what NACCB is to quality system registrars.

The qualifications and practices for quality system assessors are, as you might guess, thoroughly documented:

- ISO 10011-1, 10011-2, and 10011-3 spell out (1) the guidelines for auditing quality systems, (2) qualification criteria for quality system assessors, and (3) procedures for management of assessment programs, respectively. These guidelines apply to internal quality assessments (required by the standard) as well as to external and extrinsic quality system assessments.

- ISO Guide 48 (1986) specifies guidelines for third-party assessment and registration of a supplier's quality system.

The assessment team is made up of a *lead assessor,* who coordinates the assessment and handles relations with the facility, and one (or more, depending on facility size) other assessors. Ideally, the team includes at least one assessor who is experienced in the type of operation being assessed. Assessors must be free of any potential conflict of interest, and the facility has the right to object to the inclusion of any assessor with whom conflicts may arise.

Inspection of the Facility

Armed with their copy of the quality manual, the assessment team inspects the facility and its process. The purpose is to ensure that the quality system depicted in the manual

- Is adequate to the purposes of the process concerned
- Is capable of ensuring that output will conform to documented requirements
- Fairly represents the quality system actually being operated in the facility

First, the assessment team meets with facility management to review the assessment procedure, set up lines of communication, and resolve any open issues. Then the formal on-site assessment of the facility begins. Inspection entails:

- A detailed review of the quality system to determine the extent to which it conforms to the requirements of the standard
- Facility tours, employee interviews, and reviews of documentation, including the written procedures and operating instructions referred to in the quality manual
- Checks of critical quality system functions, such as internal audits, management reviews, corrective action, and documentation changes

In all respects, facility personnel are expected to demonstrate that the procedures documented in the quality manual are utilized in practice. The assessment is detailed, specific, and rigorous. As you have no doubt observed, ISO 9000 is no facade. There is little wiggle room and no place to hide. You must walk your talk.

As Anthony Coggeshall of Adhesives Research observes: "Good assessors spend the bulk of their time talking not to management or supervisors, but to people who do the real work. Oh, they'll talk to all the big cheeses coming in and going out, but in between they talk to the troops. Makes it hard to hide things."

The Assessment Report

At the end, the assessment team makes a verbal report of its findings to facility management. The team may point out "observations"—nonconformances of a relatively insignificant nature—as well as "minor" and "major" nonconformances. Minor nonconformances do not necessarily block registration (assuming facility management corrects them before the first semi-annual surveillance assessment is made).Major nonconformances usually halt the registration process in its tracks until they are corrected.

The assessment team issues its findings in written form as well. Included in this report are necessary corrective actions as well as a deadline for completing them. The registrar may conduct a full or partial reassessment to confirm that corrective actions have been made. These reassessments can require the payment of additional fees.

When this phase is concluded, the registrar issues a certificate of registration.

Timing and Costs

Many facility managements want to know now much ISO 9000 registration costs—and how long it takes. These are difficult questions to answer, owing to the wide variance of facilities seeking registration and the wide range of cost schedules offered by various registrars.

Generally, registration costs are scaled to facility size. For example, one British registrar charges about $10,000 for the services required to certify a facility of fewer than 100 people to ISO 9001. Facilities employing up to 500 people pay about $15,000, and those employing up to 1000 are charged about $21,000.

Another NACCB-sanctioned registrar charges $6300 to certify a facility of up to 20 people to ISO 9001, and about $17,000 for facilities of 100–200 people. All these expenses are exclusive of travel and living costs for the auditors. In addition, annual fees are required to maintain registration.

Timing is another variable issue. Generally, as of this writing, lead times from application to registration audit run 8 to 12 weeks—if all goes well. These figures can, of course, vary by facility size and the registrar's particular schedule.

Privileges of Registration

Henceforth, the facility is certified to ISO 9001, 9002, or 9003. As evidence, the facility is awarded a certificate which bears the registrar's mark, as well as the logo of the accrediting body (such as

NACCB), if applicable. The certificate also bears a unique registration number.

Now the facility can show its certificate to customers and others as evidence of the objective approval of its quality system. It can use its registration logos in advertising and other printed matter, as regulated by the specific guidelines of its registrar. Its name may also appear in published directories of registered firms that are consulted by purchasing executives in the EC and elsewhere.

After Registration

Registration is not the end of the process, only the beginning. From that point forward, the facility and the registrar are, in effect, married.

The basic elements of the relationship are:

- Payment of an annual fee
- Review and approval of quality system changes
- Semiannual surveillance assessments

Quality System Changes

As the facility and process changes, the quality system will require changes, too. Not only is change expected by ISO 9000; it is considered a virtual necessity.

The quality system's internal audit, management review, and corrective action mechanisms will generate continuous changes and improvements to specific quality system procedures. In the course of its two semiannual surveillance visits—which are, really, miniaudits of the facility—the registrar will evaluate these changes and their impact on the quality system's conformance to the standard.

Surveillance Assessments

The semiannual surveillance assessments are performed to evaluate changes to the quality system, follow up on prior corrective actions, and verify that the quality system continues to conform to requirements.

These assessments are always performed, but many registrars admit that they are "full assessments" only in unusual cases. Usually, they focus upon

- Results of past corrective actions
- Areas which have generated nonconformances in the past
- Randomly selected elements of the quality system

The assessment follows the same general routine as the registration assessment:

- Initial meeting
- Assessment
- Verbal report of findings
- Written report of findings
- Corrective action requests, with deadlines

Most facilities find these assessments to be helpful, not burdensome. "I call them assessors," says Anthony Coggeshall, "not auditors. Auditors are people who look for dirty laundry. Assessors are there to rate my program. I enjoy the assessments. They are not looking to find things wrong with my system; they are looking to improve my company."

Maintaining Registration

Registration is easy to keep, as long as the bills are paid and the quality system remains consistent with the standard. But registration can be suspended for serious nonconformances, misuse of registration logo or documents, and other significant rules violations. Suspension can last at least until the facility implements and documents corrective actions. Failure to correct serious nonconformances can result in termination of registration.

Barring these types of occurrences, most facilities find that ISO 9000 registration is easy to maintain. When fully implemented, ISO 9000 quality systems tend to become self-enforcing, self-reinforcing, and almost second nature—as central to the facility as the product or service it produces.

14
The Future of
ISO 9000

The pace at which ISO 9000 has developed is truly amazing. It was only in the late 1950s that MIL-Q-9858 was developed, the late 1960s that the British adopted DEF/STAN, the late 1970s that the British created BS 5750, and the late 1980s that ISO 9000 was first published.

Development and change will continue to be swift. As we shall see later in this chapter, TC 176, the ISO committee responsible for the standard, is in the process of implementing some relatively minor changes to that standard. Work is also proceeding on a total overhaul to be implemented by 1996.

Meanwhile, it is likely that acceptance of ISO 9000 as the definitive international quality standard will continue to expand. Broader acceptance will happen even if the European Community never fully achieves total economic or political unity—an issue that remains shrouded in doubt. Business, and businesses, national as well as multinational, need a common quality language and a level quality playing field. If ISO 9000 did not exist, someone would have to invent it.

For all its shortcomings, and despite all the misunderstanding and misinformation that is routinely published, the ISO 9000 standard is unique. It transcends products and processes, it stands above language and custom, and it rests on principles of quality management that are almost universally accepted.

In this chapter, we will peer into an informed crystal ball to predict the future of ISO 9000.

Unification of the European Community

At this point, no one can say if the EC "single market" will ever fully come to be. Even if it does not, ISO 9000 has been adopted in virtually all EC nations—as well as by most of the industrialized nations of the world. Some fear that these nations will use the standard as means of impeding U.S. imports. Whether or not that development will come to pass is another major issue, well beyond the province of this book.

But given the high level of acceptance of ISO 9000 that already exists, it only makes sense for U.S. firms which have a significant market presence in the EC to obtain whatever quality system certification domestic EC firms are expected to have. ISO 9000 registration is especially important for facilities which make products already covered by EC product directives—product certification cannot be obtained without quality system certification.

American facilities with future interests in Europe should also seriously consider obtaining ISO 9000 certification irrespective of EC unification or EC requirements. And American facilities that have no interests in the EC—and that are having problems with quality, productivity, and customer satisfaction—should consider using ISO 9000 as a quality system model in order to maintain competitiveness.

Toward an American Accreditation Body

When asked to explain his chief complaint about ISO 9000, David Turtletaub of Phillips Circuit Assembly, an ISO 9002 candidate, points to "the certification process that you have to go through, and all the political stuff behind it, the different countries and different agencies in Europe and who accepts what certification and the bureaucracy. It definitely needs to be straightened out."

Why has this not happened already? The wheels of government

grind exceedingly slowly. And it could be, as speculated by Dennis Beckley of Dayton-Rogers, that the U.S. government resists ISO 9000 because of the "NIH syndrome" (not invented here).

At Perry Johnson, Inc., we expect that to change. In the near future, we expect the U.S. government to recognize the importance of ISO 9000 to America's worldwide business interests by officially sanctioning an American organization to accredit U.S.-based registrars— on a par with the NACCB in England, RvC in the Netherlands, and others. U.S. government sanction should include some official means of certifying quality system assessors and lead assessors.

These developments will simplify the registration process in America—to a degree. The effectiveness of this step hinges on the extent to which resulting U.S. registrations are honored by EC nations. The ideal situation is for the United States to enter into reciprocal agreements with the EC, wherein registrations conferred by U.S.-accredited bodies would be recognized and accepted in the EC, and vice versa.

No one can say whether, or when, U.S. accreditation and reciprocity will happen. It is heavily dependent upon complex trade and political issues. In the meantime, the central advice given in this book should remain valid. If ISO 9000 registration is necessary, or helpful, to further your commercial interests in the EC, make sure the authority of your registrar is recognized and accepted in the EC.

Changes to the Standard

Currently, finishing touches are being placed upon a number of minor changes to the ISO standard—particularly ISO 9001 and ISO 9002. These changes are expected to be implemented by the end of 1993 and will affect quality system assessments starting in 1994.

Some changes are minor "wordsmithing" ones; others are more significant. To begin with, *section numbers* will be uniform among the three contractual models (ISO 9001, 9002, and 9003).

Servicing will be included in ISO 9002, expanding it to 19 sections rather than 18. Here is an overview of changes to specific sections.

Management Responsibility (4.1). This section has been given new language to broaden its scope:

- Management must define responsibility for people who initiate action to prevent the occurrence of *system* nonconformities, not just product nonconformities, as the section is currently written.
- The definition of management representative is tightened. The MR must be a member of facility management, not a consultant or other outsider.
- Management reviews are to be conducted at defined intervals of sufficient frequency, not simply at "appropriate intervals."

Quality System (4.2). The "notes" labeled A through G, which define the activities to be covered by the quality system, are more specifically stated as requirements. The current wording, by positioning them as notes, suggests that they are not requirements.

Contract Review (4.3). The wording is changed to make clear that the provisions apply to all forms of contract between facility and customer. They cover not just written contracts but verbal agreements and implied customer requirements up to the point of acceptance of the order.

Purchasing (4.6). This section is reworded to provide more details and guidance on how subcontractors (suppliers) are to be evaluated and selected, particularly with respect to their quality systems and quality audits.

Process Control (4.9). As currently worded, this section makes no mention of equipment maintenance. The new version makes equipment maintenance a required component of process control.

Inspection and Test Status (4.12). As currently worded, this section applies to production and installation of product. The new version expands coverage to include any servicing stage as well.

Corrective Action (4.14). As currently worded, this section applies to nonconforming product only. The new version expands coverage to apply to any nonconformance that affects the system. Thus, corrective action must be taken on nonconforming activities as well as nonconforming products. The change reinforces the philosophy of continuous improvement throughout the process.

Internal Quality Audits (4.17). The scope of internal quality audits is expanded to include audits not only of the quality system but the processes and/or the product as well.

Voices of the Users: The Future of ISO 9000

Brian Burke, Container Products Inc.:

I'm sold on ISO 9000. . . . I think that the concept of unifying all these facets of quality management and certifying the system by an objective third party is a good way to go. For us, the discipline of going through the preparation has been the most valuable thing. The registration will be neat, our commercial people will run with it, but the discipline of putting together the quality system and the documentation has been the most beneficial thing of all.

Dennis Beckley, Dayton-Rogers Corp.:

Our company has 3000 customers. This plant alone has 600. I probably undergo 20 mail-in audits and 2 on-site audits each month. I know ISO 9000 won't reduce my audit load in the near future, but in time it will. I know I'll be looking for ISO registration among my supply base, just as I look for Q1; and when my suppliers get ISO registered, I'll waive the audits.

Hopefully, as time goes by ISO 9000 will be recognized as a basic quality criterion by everyone: government, automotive, everyone. Obviously everyone has individual specs, but I think there needs to be a general quality standard that everyone adopts across the board.

Linda Kabel, Menasha Corp.:

I just hope ISO 9000 isn't just a passing fad. So many programs are here today, gone tomorrow. We're putting money and time into ISO 9000 because we think it's a good system, very in depth. Hopefully, in time, our customers will exempt us from audits, once we're registered. That would be a real time saver.

David Turtletaub, Phillips Circuit Assembly:

I think the ISO 9000 standard itself is good. I don't see much need for improvements or changes to the standards themselves. I do think the expense has to be looked at. There are smaller companies which can't afford it. And all the confusion in the U.S. marketplace now about registration bodies, who accepts what registration, how the registration is actually done—all that has to be fixed.

I think the idea of no trade barriers in Europe, and a single currency, is going to be hard to pull off because of cultural aspects—the differences in cultures and nationalities. If the EC never really gets together, ISO 9000 is going to lose some of its punch. If that happens, and the U.S. ignores ISO 9000, then it will disappear.

But the United States is still the number-one exporter in the world. I think we need to get hold of ISO 9000 and run with it, instead of just letting the EC dictate it to us. I think if we take the lead on ISO 9000, it'll take hold worldwide. It will be around for a long time.

Don Van Hook, Strahman Valves:

For one thing, I think there should be international accreditation, rather than separate accreditation for each country. I also think ISO might want to get just a little more specific in some areas and not leave so much open to interpretation. Record retention, for example. Our consultant recommended ten years. Why? Because it was a nice round number. We suggested three to five years, and he agreed that was probably adequate.

George Raub, TRW:

I'm comfortable with specifics of the standard itself. It covers the minimum kind of quality system. It ought to go more in depth on quality costs and continuous improvement, but a well-run company looks at those things whether a standard requires them or not.

The registration process needs to be cleaner. Our government needs to get treaties for cross recognition of accreditation and certification. It's a shame that our government makes it so confusing for U.S. businesses to pursue what is, after all, in the national interest: building American exports.

My fearless forecast is that the next hotbed of ISO acceptance will be the Far East. Not Japan, which is already inbred with quality circles and work groups and the like, but the Third World: India, Asia, and others.

Anthony Coggeshall, Adhesives Research, Inc.:

Looking into the future, within two years, give or take a year, you won't be able to do business in Europe without ISO 9000 registration. Within five years, you won't be able to work with a U.S. government agency, or a company supplying a government agency, without ISO 9000 certification. Within five or ten years, it'll be tough to do business in the United States without it.

Afterword

Here's one of beauties of ISO 9000. When we went to Switzerland to assist in an audit over there, we sat down with QSF [a quality systems registrar and Swiss government quality body] to talk it over. And when we started talking about the ISO 9000 standard, we understood each other perfectly. Different countries, different cultures, different businesses, but with ISO 9000 there was no misunderstanding, no misinterpretation. We were talking the same language.   *Jim Ecklein*
Augustine Medical
Registered to ISO 9003
ISO 9001 Candidate

Appendix A
ISO 9000 Cross-Reference

ISO 9001 (9004 equivalent)	9002	9003	9004	9004-2
1. Management Responsibility	1	1	4	5.2
2. Quality System Principles	2	2	5	5.4
3. Contract Review (Quality in Marketing)	3	—	7	6.1
4. Design Control (Quality in Specification and Design)	—	—	8	6.2
5. Document Control (Quality Documentation and Records)	4	3	17	5.4.3
6. Purchasing (Quality in Procurement)	5	—	9	6.2.4.3
7. Purchaser Supplied Product	6	—	—	—
8. Product Identification (Material Control) and Traceability	7	4	11.2	—
9. Process Control (Quality in Production)	8	—	10	6.3
9. Control of Production	8	—	11	
10. Inspection and Testing (Product Verification)	9	5	12	—
11. Inspection, Measuring and Test Equipment (Control of Measuring and Test Equipment)	10	6	13	—

ISO 9001 (9004 equivalent)	9002	9003	9004	9004-2
12. Inspection and Test Status (Control of Verification Status)	11	7	11.7	—
13. Control of Non-Conforming Product (Nonconformity)	12	8	14	6.3.5.2
14. Corrective Action	13	—	15	6.3.5
15. Handling, Storage, Packaging, and Delivery (Handling and Post-Production Functions)	14	9	16	6.2.4.6
16. Quality Records	15	10	17.3	5.4.3
17. Internal Quality Audits (Auditing the Quality System)	16	—	5.4	5.4.4
18. Training (Personnel)	17	11	18	5.3
19. Servicing (After-Sales Servicing)	—	—	16.2	—
20. Statistical Techniques (Use of Statistical Methods)	18	12	20	6.4.3
—. Economics—quality-related cost considerations	—	—	6	—
—. Product safety and liability	—	—	19	—

ISO 9001
Self-Assessment

Here, arranged in numerical order, are the requirements and guidelines of the 20 sections of ISO 9001. You can use this appendix to conduct an informal assessment of the conformance of your facility's quality system to the requirements of the standard.

For each requirement, indicate the level of conformance by circling the appropriate score. Enter that score in the column to the right. Total the scores for each section.

At the end of this appendix, you can total your scores and evaluate, on a general basis, how your quality system rates against the requirements of ISO 9001.

ISO 9001, Section 4.1: Management Responsibility

Components	Self-assessment			
	Strong	Mod.	Weak	Score
Management has defined and documented facility quality policy.	10	5	0	
Specific quality responsibilities of all employees are defined and documented.	10	5	0	
An organization chart exists which shows management structure and relationships.	10	5	0	
A specific entity has responsibility for providing sufficient resources and personnel to complete facility tasks.	10	5	0	
Management conducts activities to verify effectiveness of design, production, installation, and service activities.	10	5	0	
Manager responsible for verification activities has been defined; custodian of records has been specified.	10	5	0	
A management representative, with sufficient authority, has been designated to oversee conformance of quality system to the standard.	10	5	0	
Managers conduct regular review meetings to assess the quality system and ensure its continued effectiveness. Minutes of such reviews are documented and location of this documentation is specified.	10	5	0	
Procedures covering all activities specified by this section exist.	10	5	0	
			Total	

ISO 9001, Section 4.2: Quality System

Components	Self-assessment				
	Strong	Mod.	Weak	N/A	Score
Facility has prepared procedures and instructions to meet the requirements of the standard.	10	5	0	10	
Facility has effectively implemented those procedures and instructions.	10	5	0	10	
Facility should document procedures and instructions with quality plans and a quality manual.	10	5	0	10	
Facility has identified and acquired resources needed to achieve required quality levels, including equipment, material, testing and measuring methods and devices, and qualified human resources.	10	5	0	10	
Facility's monitoring and adjustment activities ensure the compatibility of design, production process, inspection and testing, installation, and associated documentation.	10	5	0	10	
Facility's system identifies acceptance criteria of all features and requirements.	10	5	0	10	
Facility monitors measurement requirements to ensure that the facility's ability to meet measurement requirements is anticipated and addressed on a timely basis.	10	5	0	10	
				Total	

ISO 9001, Section 4.3: Contract Review

Components	Self-assessment			Score
	Strong	Mod.	Weak	
Facility has defined responsibility and authority for contract review activities.	10	5	0	
Facility's contract review system ensures that customer requirements are adequately defined and documented.	10	5	0	
Facility's contract review system ensures that inconsistencies between customer requirements and facility standards are detected and resolved.	10	5	0	
Facility's contract review system ensures that facility has full capability to meet its obligations under the contract.	10	5	0	
Responsibility and authority for each step of facility's contract review system is specified by title/function.	10	5	0	
Records of contract review activities are maintained.	10	5	0	
Detailed procedures covering the systems herein are available.	10	5	0	
			Total	

ISO 9001, Section 4.4: Design Control

Components	Self-assessment			Score
	Strong	Mod.	Weak	
Facility has defined responsibility and authority for the design process. Includes references to documents listing qualifications.	10	5	0	
Facility has a system which defines the design planning and development process.	10	5	0	
Facility possesses a document which displays the relationships and interfaces among functions involved in the design process, as well as interfaces between the design process and other process elements.	10	5	0	
Sources of design input are identified. Facility creates a particular document, resulting from input sources, that crystallizes design requirements.	10	5	0	
Facility has defined its types of design output—blueprints, design checklists, etc.—and can present samples of these.	10	5	0	
Facility's system for verifying that designs meet input requirements is defined. The system includes at least two of the following methods: design reviews, qualification tests, alternative calculations, or comparison with proven designs.	10	5	0	
Facility's design review system takes into account various causes of design changes; for each, facility has a procedure for addressing, evaluating, and implementing needed changes.	10	5	0	
Detailed procedures covering the systems herein are available.	10	5	0	
			Total	

ISO 9001, Section 4.5: Document Control

Components	Self-assessment			Score
	Strong	Mod.	Weak	
Facility has defined responsibility and authority for creation, distribution, revision, and control of quality-related documents.	10	5	0	
Types of quality-related documents which are in use in facility have been identified.	10	5	0	
A procedure exists which specifies how quality-related documents are created and placed where employees who need them have access to them.	10	5	0	
A procedure exists which governs how quality-related documents are modified and approved, and specifies the ways in which obsolete editions are withdrawn and discarded. It also specifies a number of changes that can be made to a document before a complete reissue is required.	10	5	0	
A list of the current editions of all quality-related documents is maintained.	10	5	0	
Detailed procedures covering the systems herein are available.	10	5	0	
			Total	

ISO 9001, Section 4.6: Purchasing

Components	Self-assessment			Score
	Strong	Mod.	Weak	
Facility has defined responsibility and authority for purchasing activities and for quality of purchased products and services.	10	5	0	
Facility has a documented system for selecting suppliers that ensures that authorized suppliers can meet specified requirements.	10	5	0	
Facility has a procedure which specifies how purchasing data is to be communicated to suppliers in a way that precludes ambiguity or confusion.	10	5	0	
Facility has a procedure for verifying conformity of purchased products and services either at facility or at source. Such verification does not absolve suppliers of responsibility of meeting specified requirements.	10	5	0	
Detailed procedures covering the systems herein are available.	10	5	0	
			Total	

ISO 9001, Section 4.7: Purchaser-Supplied Product

Components	Strong	Mod.	Weak	N/A	Score
	Self-assessment				
Facility has defined responsibility and authority for scheduling, handling, and storage of purchaser-supplied items.	10	5	0	10	
Procedures exist for verification of incoming purchaser-supplied product to determine conformance with respect to features, quantity, and condition.	10	5	0	10	
Facility has a system for safeguarding purchaser-supplied product.	10	5	0	10	
Detailed procedures covering the requirements herein are available.	10	5	0	10	
Facility has a program of regular communication with owners of purchaser-supplied product to resolve any nonconformances.	10	5	0	10	
Detailed procedures covering the systems herein are available.	10	5	0	10	
				Total	

ISO 9001, Section 4.8: Product Identification and Traceability

Components	Self-assessment				Score
	Strong	Mod.	Weak	N/A	
Facility has defined responsibility and authority for assessing the need for product identification and traceability; if deemed appropriate, facility has defined responsibility for managing these activities.	10	5	0	10	
If appropriate, and/or if required by customer contract, procedures exist for identifying products (via tagging or other means) or services (via accompanying documentation).	10	5	0	10	
If appropriate, and/or if required by customer contract or legal mandate, procedures exist for tracing the origin, application, and/or location of output (products or services).	10	5	0	10	
Detailed procedures covering the systems herein are available.	10	5	0	10	
				Total	

ISO 9001, Section 4.9: Process Control

Components	Self-assessment				Score
	Strong	Mod.	Weak	N/A	
Facility has defined responsibility and authority for process control activities.	10	5	0	10	
Process areas having an impact on quality have been clearly defined.	10	5	0	10	
Procedures for maintaining controlled conditions in each such process area exist and are available to all affected personnel.	10	5	0	10	
Procedures governing the rigorous measurement and monitoring of special processes exist and are available to all affected personnel.	10	5	0	10	
				Total	

ISO 9001, Section 4.10: Inspection and Testing

Components	Self-assessment				Score
	Strong	Mod.	Weak	N/A	
Facility has defined responsibility and authority for receiving, in-process and final inspection and testing systems.	10	5	0	10	
Facility has a documented system for verifying that incoming products or services meet contractual requirements.	10	5	0	10	
If facility's system provides for release of supplied product subject to recall, system includes mechanism for identification, traceability, control, and recall of such products, under defined responsibility and authority.	10	5	0	10	
Facility has system which assures early recognition of nonconforming product at various vital in-process stages, and provides for identification and disposition of such materials.	10	5	0	10	
Facility has system which assures that output meets specified characteristics prior to release. System includes means for clear identification of conforming vs. nonconforming output.	10	5	0	10	
Detailed procedures covering the systems herein are available.	10	5	0	10	
				Total	

ISO 9001, Section 4.10: Inspection, Measuring, and Test Equipment

Components	Self-assessment				Score
	Strong	Mod.	Weak	N/A	
Facility has defined responsibility and authority for inspection, measuring, and test equipment.	10	5	0	10	
Facility has procedure for selecting measurements, determining accuracy required, and acquiring equipment which meets these requirements.	10	5	0	10	
Facility has system for verifying equipment needed and measurement accuracy, and for confirming that environmental conditions permit reliable use.	10	5	0	10	
Facility has system for calibration and adjustment of equipment at prescribed intervals against either nationally recognized standards or a documented benchmark, where no nationally recognized standards exist.	10	5	0	10	
Facility maintains full documentation of calibration procedures and results.	10	5	0	10	
Facility identifies all equipment with indicator of calibration status.	10	5	0	10	
Facility has system for reverifying previous inspection, measuring, and test results when equipment is found to be out of calibration.	10	5	0	10	
Facility has system for maintaining and storing equipment to ensure that accuracy and fitness for use are preserved. Includes means of protecting equipment from unauthorized adjustment.	10	5	0	10	
Detailed procedures covering the systems herein are available.	10	5	0	10	
				Total	

ISO 9001, Section 4.12: Inspection and Test Status

Components	Self-assessment				Score
	Strong	Mod.	Weak	N/A	
Facility has defined responsibility and authority for identifying inspection and test status of raw materials, supplied items, work in progress, and finished output.	10	5	0	10	
Facility has system for showing at all stages whether such items have not been inspected; been inspected and accepted; inspected and on hold awaiting resolution; or inspected and rejected.	10	5	0	10	
Detailed procedures covering the systems herein are available.	10	5	0	10	
				Total	

ISO 9001, Section 4.13: Control of Nonconforming Product

Components	Strong	Mod.	Weak	N/A	Score
	Self-assessment				
Facility has defined responsibility and authority for identifying nonconforming product, evaluating and segregating it, and disposing of it.	10	5	0	10	
Procedures exist for identifying nonconforming product and evaluating it, including identifying its source.	10	5	0	10	
Procedures exist for segregating the product to prevent inadvertent use.	10	5	0	10	
Procedures exist governing methods of disposal, including reworking to specified requirements, acceptance with or without repair by concession, modification for other use, or scrapping.	10	5	0	10	
System includes specified means of documenting all of the above.	10	5	0	10	
Detailed procedures covering the systems herein are available.	10	5	0	10	
				Total	

ISO 9001, Section 4.14: Corrective Action

Components	Self-assessment				
	Strong	Mod.	Weak	N/A	Score
Facility has defined responsibility and authority for designing, implementing, and documenting corrective actions.	10	5	0	10	
Facility has procedures for detecting causes of nonconformities, initiating corrective actions, controlling their implementation, verifying their effectiveness, and documenting procedural changes in order to prevent recurrence.	10	5	0	10	
Detailed procedures covering the systems herein are available.	10	5	0	10	
				Total	

ISO 9001, Section 4.15: Handling, Storage, Packaging, and Delivery

Components	Self-assessment				Score
	Strong	Mod.	Weak	N/A	
Facility has defined responsibility and authority for maintaining the quality of all materials during handling, storage, packaging, and delivery.	10	5	0	10	
Procedures exist for handling of materials to prevent damage or deterioration.	10	5	0	10	
Procedures exist which ensure security of storage areas to avert environmental or human damage, deterioration, or shrinkage.	10	5	0	10	
Procedures exist governing audit and assessment methods and means of documentation.	10	5	0	10	
Procedures specify handling methods to preserve materials in a state that conforms with specified requirements, and accurate marking processes to avert mishandling.	10	5	0	10	
Procedures exist controlling the delivery process, ensuring protection of the quality of materials during any type of transport, either in process or after final output.	10	5	0	10	
Detailed procedures covering the systems herein are available.	10	5	0	10	
				Total	

ISO 9001, Section 4.16: Quality Records

Components	Self-assessment				Score
	Strong	Mod.	Weak	N/A	
Facility has defined responsibility and authority for creation, maintenance, retention, and systematic disposal of quality records.	10	5	0	10	
Records exist which demonstrate effective operation of the quality system.	10	5	0	10	
Records document achievement of the required quality levels, and remedial actions taken in response to nonconformances.	10	5	0	10	
Records are readily retrievable by all authorized to use them.	10	5	0	10	
Retention times which meet all customer and/or legal or regulatory requirements are documented.	10	5	0	10	
Records are discarded on an orderly and systematic basis when documented retention intervals have passed.	10	5	0	10	
Detailed procedures covering the systems herein are available.	10	5	0	10	
				Total	

ISO 9001, Section 4.17: Internal Quality Audits

Components	Self-assessment				Score
	Strong	Mod.	Weak	N/A	
Facility has defined responsibility and authority for planning, scheduling, conducting, documenting, and benefiting from internal quality audits.	10	5	0	10	
Procedures place emphasis upon auditing areas which have critical importance to the quality system, or which have posted a history of nonconformances or other problems.	10	5	0	10	
Procedures specify the qualifications of the personnel assigned to perform internal audits.	10	5	0	10	
Procedures exist governing the conduct of internal audits, including safeguards against conflicts of interest and provision for follow-up actions.	10	5	0	10	
Results of internal audits are brought to the attention of the personnel responsible for the area audited.	10	5	0	10	
Management of audited areas is held accountable for taking corrective actions on or before specified dates.	10	5	0	10	
Detailed procedures covering the systems herein are available.	10	5	0	10	
				Total	

ISO 9001, Section 4.18: Training

Components	Strong	Mod.	Weak	N/A	Score
Facility has defined responsibility and authority for setting quality-related employment qualifications, assessing training needs, providing training, and maintaining records.	10	5	0	10	
Qualifications, in terms of education, training, and experience, exist for each position which affects quality.	10	5	0	10	
Procedures exist which provide for evaluating training needs for all quality-sensitive positions on a regular basis.	10	5	0	10	
Training programs are conducted to correct identified nonconformances in qualifications.	10	5	0	10	
Records, both individual and corporate, are maintained of all training activities.	10	5	0	10	
Detailed procedures covering the systems herein are available.	10	5	0	10	
				Total	

The column header "Self-assessment" spans Strong, Mod., Weak, and N/A.

ISO 9001, Section 4.19: Servicing

Components	Self-assessment				Score
	Strong	Mod.	Weak	N/A	
Facility has defined responsibility and authority for servicing activities.	10	5	0	10	
Facility has established and maintained procedures for performing service.	10	5	0	10	
Facility has procedures for verifying that servicing meets established customer requirements.	10	5	0	10	
Detailed procedures covering the systems herein are available.	10	5	0	10	
				Total	

ISO 9001, Section 4.20: Statistical Techniques

Components	Self-assessment				Score
	Strong	Mod.	Weak	N/A	
Facility has defined responsibility and authority for evaluating the use of statistical techniques throughout facility and process.	10	5	0	10	
Facility has procedures for assessing statistical techniques to verify (critical) product characteristics, to assess process capability, and for other purposes.	10	5	0	10	
Detailed procedures covering the systems herein are available.	10	5	0	10	
				Total	

Your ISO 9000 Self-Assessment

To get a snapshot look at how ready your quality system is for ISO 9001 certification, add together the scores from each of the 20 sections and compare your total score with the list below.

901–1200: Strong   Most elements of your system conform to the basic ISO 9000 quality system standards. Examine the areas with weak scores and implement enhancements; refer to ISO-9004 for additional guidance. It is also advisable to arrange for preassessment from an ISO 9000 registration body.

601–900: Fair   Many elements of your system conform to the basic ISO 9000 quality system standards. But a significant part of your quality system either does not conform to the standards or is not present. Pinpoint these areas and implement the systems required; for guidance, you can refer to official manuals such as ISO-9004 or acquire the services of an ISO 9000 training and consulting specialist.

301–600: Weak   Much of your quality system does not conform to the basic ISO 9000 quality system standards. A great deal of orientation and training in the specifics of the standards is necessary. If your facility is serious about ISO 9000 certification, establish a steering committee and acquire the services of an ISO 9000 training and consulting specialist.

0–300: Poor   Your quality system is practically nonexistent. It is imperative that your entire process undergo review. A thorough regimen of training in total quality management (TQM) tools and techniques is recommended, as well as ISO 9000 training and consultations, before you invest time and effort in ISO 9000 certification.

Appendix C

Sample Quality Manual

ABC Typesetting Co.	Section 0.0	Page 1 of 5
Sample Quality Manual	GENERAL	

0.1 INDEX

0.0 General
0.1 Index
0.2 Quality Policy Statement
0.3 Company Background
0.4 Amendment Record
0.5 Controlled Circulation List
1.0 Management Responsibility
2.0 Quality System
3.0 Contract Review
4.0 Design Control
5.0 Document Control
6.0 Purchasing
7.0 Purchaser-Supplied Product
8.0 Product/Service Identification and Traceability
9.0 Process Control
10.0 Inspection and Testing
11.0 Inspection, Measuring, and Test Equipment
12.0 Inspection and Test Status
13.0 Control of Nonconforming Product
14.0 Corrective Action
15.0 Handling, Storage, Packaging, and Delivery
16.0 Quality Records
17.0 Internal Quality Audits
18.0 Training
19.0 Servicing
20.0 Statistical Techniques

Prepared By	Jane Hopkins	Issue Number	3
Approved By	Damon Keith	Issue Date	7/2/93

ABC Typesetting Co.	Section 0.0	Page 2 of 5
Sample Quality Manual	GENERAL	

0.2 QUALITY POLICY STATEMENT

ABC Typesetting Co. is absolutely committed to meeting and exceeding our customers' expectations in terms of the quality of the products and the services which we provide.

I personally affirm this commitment. To bolster it, I am leading the effort to establish a quality system which will meet quality system standard ISO 9001. With this quality system, we are committing ourselves to a strategy of continuous improvement, relentlessly seeking to learn the expectations of our customers and striving to meet and exceed those expectations at every juncture.

We intend for these efforts to help us meet the following goals:

- Double our market share within five years
- Maintain our position at the cutting edge of typesetting and publishing technology
- Achieve outstanding financial performance as measured by return on investment and return on assets
- Maintain our reputation for quality products, service, and civic responsibility

The entire ABC Typesetting team must adhere to the spirit and the letter of the firm's quality policy as well as the directives of this Quality Manual and its subordinate documents. I plan to be actively involved in building this exciting new effort through membership on the Quality Steering Team as well as execution of the various responsibilities given to me in this manual.

Signed:

Wallace P. Stevens, President   February 1993

Prepared By	W. Stevens	Issue Number	3
Approved By	W. Stevens	Issue Date	7/2/93

ABC Typesetting Co.	Section 0.0	Page 3 of 5
Sample Quality Manual	GENERAL	

0.3   COMPANY BACKGROUND

ABC Typesetting Co. was founded by Wallace Stevens in North Fork (L.I.), New York, in 1969. From a single-person entrepreneurship it has grown to encompass a 20,000-square-foot plant employing the latest in computer-driven typesetting systems. ABC now also has a printing division, direct mail division, and telemarketing services division.

ABC's major clients are Manhattan-based advertising agencies and, to an extent, their clients. Through aggressive marketing and unparalleled service—the company's motto is "Whatever It Takes"—ABC has transformed what is normally an adversarial agency/vendor environment into one of partnership and fulfillment of shared goals. Indeed, ABC's clients are its partners and its partners are its clients.

Prepared By	Clark Hunnert	Issue Number	3
Approved By	Damon Keith	Issue Date	7/2/93

ABC Typesetting Co.	Section 0.0	Page 4 of 5
Sample Quality Manual	GENERAL	

0.4 AMENDMENT RECORD

This manual may contain only the pages issued by the facility. The Management Representative will process all authorized changes, insert amended pages into official distribution copies, and see to it that obsolete pages are withdrawn and destroyed. The Master Copy of this Quality Manual, kept in the custody of the Management Representative's office, shall be the final authority as to amendment status for all sections in the manual.

Date	Section page	Details	Signature

Prepared By	Grace Wichens	Issue Number	3
Approved By	Damon Keith	Issue Date	7/2/93

ABC *Typesetting Co.*	Section 0.0	Page 5 of 5
Sample Quality Manual	GENERAL	

0.5 CONTROLLED CIRCULATION LIST

Copy No.   Copy Custodian

1	President
2	Senior Vice President
3	Vice President—Typesetting
4	Vice President—Direct Marketing
5	Vice President—Telemarketing
6	Vice President—Client Services
7	Director of Administration
8	Director of Finance
9	Director of Planning
10	Director of Marketing
11	Director of Quality
12	Director of Human Resources
13	Accreditation Body

Prepared By	Mary Eddy	Issue Number	3
Approved By	Damon Keith	Issue Date	7/2/93

ABC Typesetting Co.	Section 1.0	Page 1 of 2
Sample Quality Manual	MANAGEMENT RESPONSIBILITY	

1.1 SCOPE

The system described in this section of the Quality Manual complies with the requirements of the Standard:

Paragraph 4.1: Management Responsibility

The section describes the responsibility, authority, and management structure of the facility.

1.2 RESPONSIBILITY AND AUTHORITY

The President has ultimate responsibility for the facility's products and services. He or she is also responsible for setting the facility's quality policy.

The Corporate Steering Team advises and monitors the establishment and implementation of the quality system.

Directors, managers, supervisors, and team leaders are responsible for implementing the quality programs promulgated by the quality system and quality policy. They, as well as all facility employees, are responsible for the quality of the products and services under their control.

1.3 VERIFICATION OF RESOURCES AND PERSONNEL

The Corporate Steering Team is chaired by the Senior Vice President and attended by designated members. The team is responsible for providing adequate resources and assigning qualified personnel to all activities.

Prepared By	Jane Quigley	Issue Number	3
Approved By	Damon Keith	Issue Date	7/2/93

ABC *Typesetting Co.*	Section 1.0	Page 2 of 2
Sample Quality Manual	MANAGEMENT RESPONSIBILITY	

Verification activities, including internal quality audits, are carried out at the direction of the Corporate Steering Team by personnel independent of those responsible for the activities being audited.

1.4 MANAGEMENT REPRESENTATIVE

The Corporate Quality Manager also functions as the facility's Management Representative. He or she has sufficient authority to ensure that the requirements of ISO 9001 (1987) are maintained. In the absence of the Management Representative, a qualified deputy is appointed.

The Management Representative, or his or her deputy, is responsible to the Corporate Steering Team for the effective operation of the quality system.

1.5 MANAGEMENT REVIEW

Regular review meetings, chaired by the Senior Vice President, are held to monitor the effectiveness of the quality system, to agree upon corrective action, and to review the effectiveness of prior corrective actions. These meetings are attended by the Corporate Steering Team and the Director of Quality.

Meeting minutes are kept and circulated among attendees. Meetings are conducted by agenda, a current sample of which is included in operational procedures.

1.6 RELATED DOCUMENTATION

Details of the approved methods are contained in:

OP-01: Management Responsibility, Appendix 1: Plant Organization/Job Responsibilities

Prepared By	Jane Quigley	Issue Number	3
Approved By	Damon Keith	Issue Date	7/2/93

ABC Typesetting Co.	Section 2.0	Page 1 of 2
Sample Quality Manual	QUALITY SYSTEM	

2.1 SCOPE

The system described in this section of the Quality Manual complies with the requirements of the Standard:

Paragraph 4.2: Quality System

The section describes the responsibility, authority, and management of the facility's quality policy.

2.2 RESPONSIBILITY AND AUTHORITY

Directors, managers, supervisors, and employees are obligated to work in accordance with the specific requirements of the documented quality system.

2.3 QUALITY SYSTEM

All quality-related activities are governed by procedures and written instructions. Within the quality system, emphasis is placed upon the following:

- Prevention versus detection
- Selection, monitoring, and control of suppliers
- Procedures ensuring the safe handling, packaging, storage, and delivery of products to customers
- Establishment of appropriate acceptability standards at specified process points
- Procedures to establish and monitor process capability
- Regular internal audit and review
- Effective corrective action procedures for dealing with client complaints and other instances of nonconformance

Prepared By	Willem Cathert	Issue Number	3
Approved By	Damon Keith	Issue Date	7/2/93

ABC Typesetting Co.	Section 2.0	Page 2 of 2
Sample Quality Manual	QUALITY SYSTEM	

- Effective management of measuring and test equipment
- Use of appropriate statistical techniques

2.4 RELATED DOCUMENTATION

The documented quality system is made up of the Quality Manual, operational procedures, work instructions, and specific instruction manuals. Procedures are circulated for use by management and employees as needed.

Details of the approved methods are contained in:

OP-2: Quality System Documentation Procedures

Prepared By	Willem Cathert	Issue Number	3
Approved By	Damon Keith	Issue Date	7/2/93

ABC Typesetting Co.	Section 3.0	Page 1 of 2
Sample Quality Manual	CONTRACT REVIEW	

3.1 SCOPE

The system described in this section of the Quality Manual complies with the requirements of the Standard:

Paragraph 4.3: Contract Review

The section describes the method used by the facility for the review and verification of contracts, including the availability of resources and the facility's capacity to meet client requirements.

3.2 RESPONSIBILITY AND AUTHORITY

Account executives provide the Client Project Data Sheet (CPDS) for each client project.

Account Services is responsible for contract review, planning, and scheduling of production, in accordance with the CPDS.

The Account Services Manager approves all original CPDS documents and any subsequent CPDS documents with specific changes.

3.3 QUALITY ACTIVITY

The CPDS is the complete agreement with the client as to the scope, nature, and specifics of the project. It includes an estimate of costs. CPDSs must be signed by an authorized client representative and countersigned by the account executive before submission to the Account Services Manager.

Any discrepancies which may arise are resolved by the Account Services Team in consultation with the client. All approved changes must be notated on the CPDS and signed by account executive and client.

Prepared By	Roger Dinemann	Issue Number	3
Approved By	Damon Keith	Issue Date	7/2/93

ABC Typesetting Co.	Section 3.0	Page 2 of 2
Sample Quality Manual	CONTRACT REVIEW	

Signature by client on a CPDS comprises project production release. Schedules are prepared and reviewed to confirm the availability of needed internal and external resources to meet client requirements. Schedule is updated regularly and is subject to regular review by Account Services Manager prior to release.

Records of all project and contract activities are maintained.

3.4 RELATED DOCUMENTATION

Details of the approved methods are contained in:

OP-3: Contract Review

Prepared By	Roger Dinemann	Issue Number	3
Approved By	Damon Keith	Issue Date	7/2/93

ABC Typesetting Co.	Section 4.0	Page 1 of 2
Sample Quality Manual	DESIGN CONTROL	

4.1 SCOPE

The system described in this section of the Quality Manual complies with the requirements of the Standard:

Paragraph 4.4: Design Control

The section describes the system used by the facility to ensure that output (products and services) meets client requirements.

4.2 RESPONSIBILITY AND AUTHORITY

The Client Services Manager has ultimate responsibility for design control. The supervisors of various departments involved in the design process—including Copy, Type, Graphics, EDP, and Fulfillment—are responsible for carrying out their portion of the documented design process, as specified in procedures and work instructions.

4.3 QUALITY ACTIVITY

The supervisors of Copy, Type, Graphics, EDP, and Fulfillment comprise a Design Control Team. This team is the interface among these departments.

Design input is provided in the form of a Client Project Data Sheet (CPDS). Collectively, the team prepares design plans in response to the requirements of the CPDS. These plans are reviewed with the account executive and countersigned by the Account Services Manager to verify that output meets the input requirements prior to presentation to the client. Verification may be by means of design reviews, audit by disinterested parties, or comparison with past projects for the same or similar clients.

Prepared By	B. Halliburton	Issue Number	3
Approved By	Damon Keith	Issue Date	7/2/93

ABC Typesetting Co.	Section 4.0	Page 2 of 2
Sample Quality Manual	DESIGN CONTROL	

4.4 RELATED DOCUMENTATION

Details of the approved methods are contained in:

OP-4: Design Control

Prepared By	B. Halliburton	Issue Number	3
Approved By	Damon Keith	Issue Date	7/2/93

ABC Typesetting Co.	Section 5.0	Page 1 of 2
Sample Quality Manual	DOCUMENT CONTROL	

5.1 SCOPE

The system described in this section of the Quality Manual complies with the requirements of the Standard:

Paragraph 4.5: Document Control

The section describes the manner in which all quality system documentation is controlled.

5.2 RESPONSIBILITY AND AUTHORITY

The Corporate Steering Team is responsible for review and approval of changes to the documented quality system. The Senior Vice President and Management Representative also approve all changes. The Management Representative is responsible for document control.

5.3 QUALITY ACTIVITY

The quality system is documented by the Quality Manual, operational procedures, work instructions, and specific quality manuals.

These documents are generated on a documented basis by specified persons in the departments concerned. All are approved by the Corporate Steering Team and Management Representative prior to issue. A procedure ensures that the latest issue of all documents is available at all locations where needed.

Changes to quality-related documents are reviewed by the Management Representative and submitted to the Corporate Steering Team

Prepared By	Ben Scribner	Issue Number	3
Approved By	Damon Keith	Issue Date	7/2/93

ABC Typesetting Co.	Section 5.0	Page 2 of 2
Sample Quality Manual	DOCUMENT CONTROL	

for approval. This body reviews proposed changes for intrinsic effect as well as for corollary effect on the facility's process. After review and approval, the President approves all changes and modifications. After a document has been subject to three changes, it must undergo a complete review and reissue.

All changes are recorded. Revised documents are clearly identified as such. A master list shows the current revisions of all quality documentation. Procedures ensure the prompt disposal of obsolete documents.

5.4 RELATED DOCUMENTATION

Details of the approved methods are contained in:

OP-5: Approval, Issue, and Change of Documents

Prepared By	Ben Scribner	Issue Number	3
Approved By	Damon Keith	Issue Date	7/2/93

ABC Typesetting Co.	Section 6.0	Page 1 of 2
Sample Quality Manual	PURCHASING	

6.1 SCOPE

The system described in this section of the Quality Manual complies with the requirements of the Standard:

Paragraph 4.6: Purchasing

The section describes the way in which suppliers of material and subcontract services are selected, approved, and controlled.

6.2 RESPONSIBILITY AND AUTHORITY

Internal Accounting is responsible for the ordering and release of materials from designated vendors. Account Services is responsible for selection and management of contract service providers. Quality is responsible for certification of product and service suppliers.

6.3 QUALITY ACTIVITY

The facility has implemented procedures in all areas to ensure the conformance of purchased items to requirements. Production materials, components, and equipment are purchased from approved vendors. Service suppliers are certified to one or more of a number of published expertise categories prior to engagement.

Supplier Certification Program

There are three types of product or service providers: (a) approved, (b) qualified, and (c) certified. Approved providers are selected on the basis of an initial survey. All product or service supplied by this level is subject to incoming audit.

Prepared By	Dale Polewach	Issue Number	3
Approved By	Damon Keith	Issue Date	7/2/93

ABC Typesetting Co.	Section 6.0	Page 2 of 2
Sample Quality Manual	PURCHASING	

   Qualified suppliers have undergone and passed a formal audit of experience and activity encompassing at least six months. Criteria include providing acceptable levels of performance in terms of quality, cost, delivery, and service. Products and services from qualified suppliers are subject only to limited levels of incoming inspection and review.
   Certified suppliers have demonstrated the ability to meet specified criteria over a period exceeding no less than one year. They have also passed a certification audit. Incoming products and services from certified suppliers are subject only to random audits.

Performance of all suppliers is tracked on an ongoing basis and a master list is maintained of supplier status.

6.4 PURCHASE ORDERS

Purchase orders are clearly identified and either state specifications and requirements explicitly or make clear and unequivocal reference to associated specifications and requirements.

6.5 RELATED DOCUMENTATION

Details of the approved methods are contained in:

   OP-6: Supplier Selection, Certification, and Control

Prepared By	Dale Polewach	Issue Number	3
Approved By	Damon Keith	Issue Date	7/2/93

ABC *Typesetting Co.*	Section 7.0	Page 1 of 1
Sample Quality Manual	CLIENT-SUPPLIED PRODUCT	

7.1 SCOPE

The system described in this section of the Quality Manual complies with the requirements of the Standard:

Paragraph 4.7: Purchaser-Supplied Product

The section describes the methods used to verify, store, and maintain client-supplied products.

7.2 RESPONSIBILITY AND AUTHORITY

Account Services is responsible for scheduling, handling, and storage of client-supplied items.

7.3 QUALITY ACTIVITY

Client-supplied items include artwork, supplied direct mail pieces, sample products, and miscellaneous items. These are treated as if they were purchased items and carefully protected in accordance with procedure. They are also subject to verification upon receipt. Nonconformances are so identified and held for review with client prior to use.

7.4 RELATED DOCUMENTATION

Details of the approved methods are contained in:

OP-7: Client-Supplied Product

Prepared By	H. C. Keefe	Issue Number	3
Approved By	Damon Keith	Issue Date	7/2/93

ABC *Typesetting Co.*	Section 8.0	Page 1 of 2
Sample Quality Manual	PRODUCT/SERVICE IDENTIFICATION AND TRACEABILITY	

8.1 SCOPE

The system described in this section of the Quality Manual complies with the requirements of the Standard:

Paragraph 4.8: Product Identification and Traceability

The section describes how products and services (output) are identified throughout the production process.

8.2 RESPONSIBILITY AND AUTHORITY

Account Services and Production are responsible for ensuring that all materials and documentation associated with client projects are clearly marked for identification and traceability. Production is responsible for maintaining production records and Accounting is responsible for maintaining identification and traceability records. Purchasing is responsible for traceability of purchased products and services.

8.3 QUALITY ACTIVITY

All clients are identified with a unique Client Number (CN). Projects associated with each client are identified with a Project Number (PN), a unique number consisting of the Client Number plus a serial number. This PN appears on all materials, documentation, and communication relating to the project, ensuring traceability to the client and to the project.

Prepared By	Edith Eggbert	Issue Number	3
Approved By	Damon Keith	Issue Date	7/2/93

ABC Typesetting Co.	Section 8.0	Page 2 of 2
Sample Quality Manual	PRODUCT/SERVICE IDENTIFICATION AND TRACEABILITY	

Tracer numbers are assigned to purchased product. These are appended cross-laterally to client records and purchasing records so that purchased product can be traced to client projects and vice versa.

Records exist of all identification and traceability activities.

8.4   RELATED DOCUMENTATION

Details of the approved methods are contained in:

OP-8: Identification and Traceability

Prepared By	Edith Eggbert	Issue Number	3
Approved By	Damon Keith	Issue Date	7/2/93

ABC Typesetting Co.	Section 9.0	Page 1 of 2
Sample Quality Manual	PROCESS CONTROL	

9.1 SCOPE

The system described in this section of the Quality Manual complies with the requirements of the Standard:

Paragraph 4.9: Process Control

The section describes how processes are carried out under controlled conditions.

9.2 RESPONSIBILITY AND AUTHORITY

The President has overall responsibility for control of the process which produces products and services (output). Account Services is responsible for control of production planning and scheduling. Department heads are responsible for producing to the overall production plan and maintaining the required standards of excellence at all times. All employees are responsible for the quality of their work and for working in accordance with written procedures at all times.

9.3 QUALITY ACTIVITY

Production is scheduled and planned according to client needs. Written instructions for the control of all operations are specified in work instructions and operations manuals and are internally controlled documents. These contain necessary standards of work quality, specifications for materials, critical process measurement points, and measurement standards. Emphasis is placed upon prevention versus detection methods.

Prepared By	Mel Blanck	Issue Number	3
Approved By	Damon Keith	Issue Date	7/2/93

ABC Typesetting Co.	Section 9.0	Page 2 of 2
Sample Quality Manual	PROCESS CONTROL	

Production operations are carried out only by personnel who have met specific training and other qualifications. Equipment used in production processes is acquired and maintained according to plans which include verification that equipment is capable of producing to required standards.

The production schedule and supporting documentation contain all information needed to enable the facility to produce to the output specifications mandated by client and by internally generated standards.

At the end of each day, a production report is completed which details projects completed, materials used, and downtime.

9.4   RELATED DOCUMENTATION

Details of the approved methods are contained in:

OP-9: Process Control

Prepared By	Mel Blanck	Issue Number	3
Approved By	Damon Keith	Issue Date	7/2/93

ABC Typesetting Co.	Section 10.0	Page 1 of 2
Sample Quality Manual	INSPECTION AND TESTING	

10.1 SCOPE

The system described in this section of the Quality Manual complies with the requirements of the Standard:

Paragraph 4.10: Inspection and Testing

The section describes the methods used for inspection and testing.

10.2 RESPONSIBILITY AND AUTHORITY

Quality has overall responsibility for ensuring that receiving, in-process, and final inspection of products and services is performed. Shipping/Receiving is responsible for receiving, verification, and safe handling of certain items. Account Services carries out in-process inspection and testing as specified.

10.3 QUALITY ACTIVITY

Incoming materials are inspected for conformance to requirements. Accepted products are tagged and released to Account Services for use. Nonconforming items are tagged with the appropriate RETURN TO VENDOR notice, held in a designated storage area, and recorded.

Within process, inspections and tests are carried out to ensure that work standards are verified and that output meets specified standards at key process points. Results of inspection and test activities are recorded and reviewed. Nonconforming output is clearly identified and segregated from other products.

Prepared By	W. Ingersoll	Issue Number	3
Approved By	Damon Keith	Issue Date	7/2/93

ABC *Typesetting Co.*	Section 10.0	Page 2 of 2
Sample Quality Manual	INSPECTION AND TESTING	

Final output is 100 percent reviewed by specified personnel, independent of production, according to procedure. Nonconforming or questionable output is clearly identified and is not released to client without authorization from the Management Representative.

10.4 RELATED DOCUMENTATION

Details of the approved methods are contained in:

OP-10: Inspection and Testing

Prepared By	W. Ingersoll	Issue Number	3
Approved By	Damon Keith	Issue Date	7/2/93

ABC Typesetting Co.	Section 11.0	Page 1 of 2
Sample Quality Manual	INSPECTION, MEASURING, AND TEST EQUIPMENT	

11.1 SCOPE

The system described in this section of the Quality Manual complies with the requirements of the Standard:

Paragraph 4.11: Inspection, Measuring, and Test Equipment

The section describes how the inspection, measuring, and test equipment used to maintain quality and to make acceptance/rejection decisions is controlled and calibrated.

11.2 RESPONSIBILITY AND AUTHORITY

Quality is responsible for the control and calibration of the inspection, measuring, and test equipment.

11.3 QUALITY ACTIVITY

Equipment used to make in-process measurements and to make acceptance/rejection decisions is maintained in a known state of calibration.

By procedure, such equipment is checked on a regular basis against documented national standards of certification. Equipment found to be out of calibration is withdrawn from use until corrected, retested, and found acceptable. All calibration activity, including action taken in event of nonconformance, is fully documented, and each item is tagged with an indicator to show its calibration status. Calibration records are held on file for the life of the equipment.

Prepared By	Anne Marie Smith	Issue Number	3
Approved By	Damon Keith	Issue Date	7/2/93

ABC Typesetting Co.	Section 11.0	Page 2 of 2
Sample Quality Manual	INSPECTION, MEASURING, AND TEST EQUIPMENT	

Equipment subject to tampering is rendered tamperproof.

11.4 RELATED DOCUMENTATION

Details of the approved methods are contained in:

OP-11: Inspection, Measuring, and Test Equipment

Prepared By	Anne Marie Smith	Issue Number	3
Approved By	Damon Keith	Issue Date	7/2/93

ABC Typesetting Co.	Section 12.0	Page 1 of 2
Sample Quality Manual	INSPECTION AND TEST STATUS	

12.1 SCOPE

The system described in this section of the Quality Manual complies with the requirements of the Standard:

Paragraph 4.12: Inspection and Test Status

The section describes the method used to indicate the inspection and test status of supplied products or services, work in process, and finished output.

12.2 RESPONSIBILITY AND AUTHORITY

Shipping/Receiving is responsible for ensuring that supplied products or services are identified. Production and Account Services are responsible for ensuring the inspection and test status identification of work in process and final output.

12.3 QUALITY ACTIVITY

Supplied items, except those from certified suppliers (which are released immediately upon verification of features and count) are separately tagged with NOT FOR USE tags until inspection procedures are carried out. Supplied items found to be nonconforming are tagged with this status and segregated until return to supplier as an additional safeguard against inadvertent release for use.

In-process output carries an inspection/test status stamp which is cumulatively signed at specified checkpoints throughout the process. Each such approval permits the output to advance to the next process step. Output found to be nonconforming at any point is given a

Prepared By	Herc Odonton	Issue Number	3
Approved By	Damon Keith	Issue Date	7/2/93

ABC Typesetting Co.	Section 12.0	Page 2 of 2
Sample Quality Manual	INSPECTION AND TEST STATUS	

HOLD tag and segregated from the process until final determination is made. Depending upon the outcome, such output may be tagged HOLD FOR REWORK, MAKE OVER, or CANCEL. Output in either of the last two categories is physically segregated from the process to prevent its inadvertent release to the client.

Finished output undergoes final inspection and approval. No finished product is released to clients until the final APPROVED stamp has been obtained and signed by authorized personnel. Nonconforming output is physically segregated to prevent inadvertent release to the client.

Client returns are so tagged and segregated until final disposition.

12.4 RELATED DOCUMENTATION

Details of the approved methods are contained in:

OP-12: Inspection and Test Status

Prepared By	Herc Odonton	Issue Number	3
Approved By	Damon Keith	Issue Date	7/2/93

ABC Typesetting Co.	Section 13.0	Page 1 of 2
Sample Quality Manual	CONTROL OF NONCONFORMING PRODUCT	

13.1 SCOPE

The system described in this section of the Quality Manual complies with the requirements of the Standard:

Paragraph 4.13: Control of Nonconforming Product

The section describes assurance that products or services, both supplied and output, which do not conform to specified requirements are prevented from inadvertent use.

13.2 RESPONSIBILITY AND AUTHORITY

Shipping/Receiving identifies, reviews, and disposes of nonconforming supplied products or services. Production and Account Services identify, review, and dispose of nonconforming output. Ultimately the President is responsible for review and disposition of such output.

13.3 QUALITY ACTIVITY

Procedures exist for preventing inadvertent use of nonconforming products or services. Supplied products or services may be reworked, reworked by concession with supplier, or rejected and returned. Procedures also exist which prevent inadvertent use of nonconforming output. These procedures result in its being reworked to specified standards, accepted by the client with concessions, or rejected and scrapped.

Nonconforming products or services, whether supplied, within process, final output, or in the form of client returns, are clearly marked and segregated, where possible, by location.

Prepared By	R. Dean Taylor	Issue Number	3
Approved By	Damon Keith	Issue Date	7/2/93

ABC *Typesetting Co.*	Section 13.0	Page 2 of 2
Sample Quality Manual	CONTROL OF NONCONFORMING PRODUCT	

The procedure for handling nonconforming product includes determination as to causes and development and implementation of corrective actions. These activities and their effectiveness are reviewed and discussed in regular management review meetings.

13.4 RELATED DOCUMENTATION

Details of the approved methods are contained in:

OP-13: Control of Nonconforming Product

Prepared By	R. Dean Taylor	Issue Number	3
Approved By	Damon Keith	Issue Date	7/2/93

ABC *Typesetting Co.*	Section 14.0	Page 1 of 2
Sample Quality Manual	CORRECTIVE ACTION	

14.1 SCOPE

The system described in this section of the Quality Manual complies with the requirements of the Standard:

Paragraph 4.14: Corrective Action

The section describes the procedures used to correct nonconformance of products or services and noncompliances with the facility's quality system.

14.2 RESPONSIBILITY AND AUTHORITY

Department heads are responsible for implementing agreed-upon corrective actions. The Corporate Steering Team is responsible for oversight and documentation of these activities.

14.3 QUALITY ACTIVITY

Nonconformances and noncompliances may be identified by means of regular audits, internal audits, checks, tests, measurements, or personal observations.

Nonconformances and noncompliances are investigated by personnel designated for this purpose under the aegis of the department head involved. These individuals formulate and implement corrective actions and investigate the effectiveness of such corrective actions. Department heads document all corrective actions, detailing the problem, the nature of the nonconformance, the corrective action taken, and the result. These are reported to the Corporate Steering Team and the Management Representative.

Prepared By	Tommy Harris	Issue Number	3
Approved By	Damon Keith	Issue Date	7/2/93

ABC Typesetting Co.	Section 14.0	Page 2 of 2
Sample Quality Manual	CORRECTIVE ACTION	

Corrective actions which identify a need for changes to the documented quality system are addressed by the Quality Steering Team and system changes are formulated and implemented under the direction of that body, with the approval of the President, within a specified time.

14.4   RELATED DOCUMENTATION

Details of the approved methods are contained in:

OP-14: Corrective Action

Prepared By	Tommy Harris	Issue Number	3
Approved By	Damon Keith	Issue Date	7/2/93

ABC *Typesetting Co.*	Section 15.0	Page 1 of 2
Sample Quality Manual	HANDLING STORAGE, PACKAGING, AND DELIVERY	

15.1 SCOPE

The system described in this section of the Quality Manual complies with the requirements of the Standard:

Paragraph 4.15: Handling, Storage, Packaging, and Delivery

The section describes the manner in which all materials and products are handled, stored, packed, and delivered.

15.2 RESPONSIBILITY AND AUTHORITY

Shipping/Receiving is responsible for preserving the quality of received or stored materials and for the safe packaging and delivery of finished output. Production is responsible for the safety and protection of products within the process.

15.3 QUALITY ACTIVITY

Procedures specify the means for the handling, storage, packaging, and delivery of materials, in-process products, and finished output.

Procedures are implemented to prevent damage or other loss to materials, products, and output by movement, storage, or nefarious means while on the facility's site. Access to stored products is limited to authorized personnel. The environment of storage areas is regularly assessed to minimize the risk of environmental damage to stored items. Audits are regularly conducted to verify counts.

Prepared By	R. J. Duff	Issue Number	3
Approved By	Damon Keith	Issue Date	7/2/93

ABC Typesetting Co.	Section 15.0	Page 2 of 2
Sample Quality Manual	HANDLING STORAGE, PACKAGING, AND DELIVERY	

Product or service packaging instructions are part of client contracts, and these activities are carried out in accordance with the contracts. Delivery means is, likewise, agreed upon with client; packaging methods take delivery methods into account to ensure that finished output is delivered in a state of total conformance with requirements.

15.4   RELATED DOCUMENTATION

Details of the approved methods are contained in:

OP-15: Handling, Storage, Packaging, and Delivery

Prepared By	R. J. Duff	Issue Number	3
Approved By	Damon Keith	Issue Date	7/2/93

ABC Typesetting Co.	Section 16.0	Page 1 of 2
Sample Quality Manual	QUALITY RECORDS	

16.1 SCOPE

The system described in this section of the Quality Manual complies with the requirements of the Standard:

Paragraph 4.16: Quality Records

The section describes the system for retaining the records essential to demonstrating the successful operation of the facility's quality system and remedial actions taken to correct nonconformances.

16.2 RESPONSIBILITY AND AUTHORITY

The Management Representative has overall responsibility for the retention and maintenance of the facility's quality records. The Corporate Steering Team and Management Representative are responsible for specifying what records are needed to document conformance to the operative quality systems standard and to client requirements, in addition to those specified by various sections of the Quality Manual. Procedures specify all personnel with authorized access to retained quality records.

16.3 QUALITY ACTIVITY

Procedures outline the quality records to be retained, the retention intervals, the custodial locations, and disposal methods.

Unless otherwise stated, all quality records are retained for three years. Customers are permitted access to quality records where provision is made in approved contracts.

Prepared By	Bert Hengfill	Issue Number	3
Approved By	Damon Keith	Issue Date	7/2/93

ABC Typesetting Co.	Section 16.0	Page 2 of 2
Sample Quality Manual	QUALITY RECORDS	

16.4   RELATED DOCUMENTATION

Details of the approved methods are contained in:

OP-16: Quality Records

Prepared By	Bert Hengfill	Issue Number	3
Approved By	Damon Keith	Issue Date	7/2/93

ABC *Typesetting Co.*	Section 17.0	Page 1 of 2
Sample Quality Manual	INTERNAL QUALITY AUDITS	

17.1 SCOPE

The system described in this section of the Quality Manual complies with the requirements of the Standard:

Paragraph 4.17: Internal Quality Audits

The section describes the means by which the overall performance and correct operation of the documented quality system is verified by audit.

17.2 RESPONSIBILITY AND AUTHORITY

The Management Representative is responsible for planning and controlling the internal quality audit program. Qualified auditors are given audit responsibilities in areas of the facility over which they have no direct responsibility. The Corporate Steering Team reviews audit reports. Department heads are responsible for implementing agreed-upon corrective actions.

17.3 QUALITY ACTIVITY

Every element of the documented quality system undergoes a complete audit within each 12-month period. Process areas which have greater than average impact upon quality, and/or which have a documented history of frequent discrepancies and/or nonconformances, are audited more frequently. These audits are conducted in accordance with a documented procedure, the objective being to ensure continued effectiveness of the documented quality system.

Prepared By	J. M. Spector	Issue Number	3
Approved By	Damon Keith	Issue Date	7/2/93

ABC *Typesetting Co.*	Section 17.0	Page 2 of 2
Sample Quality Manual	INTERNAL QUALITY AUDITS	

Results of internal quality audits are recorded on a standard report form. This form specifies nonconformances found, agreed-upon corrective actions, individuals responsible, and time schedules for completion. Audit reports are reviewed by the Corporate Steering Team, which formulates and oversees implementation of corrective actions by affected department heads within specified time periods.

Audit records are retained for specified periods.

17.4 RELATED DOCUMENTATION

Details of the approved methods are contained in:

OP-17: Internal Quality Audits

Prepared By	J. M. Spector	Issue Number	3
Approved By	Damon Keith	Issue Date	7/2/93

ABC Typesetting Co.	Section 18.0	Page 1 of 2
Sample Quality Manual	TRAINING	

18.1 SCOPE

The system described in this section of the Quality Manual complies with the requirements of the Standard:

Paragraph 4.18: Training

The section describes the method used by the facility to ensure that all positions which have an effect upon quality are filled by personnel with appropriate experience, qualifications, and quality training.

18.2 RESPONSIBILITY AND AUTHORITY

Department heads are responsible for creating job descriptions which specify experience levels and qualifications for all positions which have an effect upon quality. Personnel is responsible for reviewing training needs, preparing training plans, documenting training courses, and maintaining training records. All managers and supervisors are responsible for establishing and maintaining quality training programs appropriate for employees under their supervision.

18.3 QUALITY ACTIVITY

Procedures govern the creation and review of quality-related job descriptions and work procedures to identify employment prerequisites and identify the facility's training needs. Employment of qualified staff is achieved by a comprehensive recruitment and selection procedure, supplemented by on the job training, internal lectures, and special courses.

Records of all courses attended by staff are maintained by Personnel for a minimum of three years.

Prepared By	Barry P. Dagogic	Issue Number	3
Approved By	Damon Keith	Issue Date	7/2/93

ABC Typesetting Co.	Section 18.0	Page 2 of 2
Sample Quality Manual	TRAINING	

18.4   RELATED DOCUMENTATION

Details of the approved methods are contained in:

OP-18: Training

Prepared By	Barry P. Dagogic	Issue Number	3
Approved By	Damon Keith	Issue Date	7/2/93

ABC *Typesetting Co.*	Section 19.0	Page 1 of 2
Sample Quality Manual	SERVICING	

19.1 SCOPE

The system described in this section of the Quality Manual complies with the requirements of the Standard:

Paragraph 4.19: Servicing

This section describes the method used to carry out postsale servicing in a manner that meets or exceeds client requirements.

19.2 RESPONSIBILITY AND AUTHORITY

Account Services is responsible for carrying out the facility's servicing policy. The Corporate Steering Team reviews servicing feedback activities and initiates creation and implementation of remedies to detected nonconformances. The President has ultimate responsibility for client satisfaction.

19.3 QUALITY ACTIVITY

Procedures exist which specify the steps required to ensure successful posttransaction servicing. Steps include prompt client recontact, elicitation of feedback, and preparation of feedback reports which provide for descriptions of reported nonconformances, actions taken, personnel responsible, and time frames. Feedback reports are regularly reviewed by the Corporate Steering Team, which may adjust the quality system to correct and prevent nonconformances in servicing or other areas of customer satisfaction.

Records of all servicing activities are maintained by Account Services in the client files for a period of one year.

Prepared By	Ginger Lake	Issue Number	3
Approved By	Damon Keith	Issue Date	7/2/93

ABC Typesetting Co.	Section 19.0	Page 2 of 2
Sample Quality Manual	SERVICING	

19.4 RELATED DOCUMENTATION

Details of the approved methods are contained in:

OP-19: Servicing

Prepared By	Ginger Lake	Issue Number	3
Approved By	Damon Keith	Issue Date	7/2/93

ABC Typesetting Co.	Section 20.0	Page 1 of 2
Sample Quality Manual	STATISTICAL TECHNIQUES	

20.1   SCOPE

The system described in this section of the Quality Manual complies with the requirements of the Standard:

Paragraph 4.20: Statistical Techniques

This section describes the system used to assess needs, and to select, implement, and use statistical techniques to monitor the effectiveness of the quality system.

20.2   RESPONSIBILITY AND AUTHORITY

The Corporate Steering Team identifies the need for specific statistical techniques. Department heads implement statistical techniques, generate reports, and utilize this information in managing their areas of operation of the quality system.

20.3   QUALITY ACTIVITY

The Corporate Steering Team identifies key process characteristics for monitoring. These are characteristics indicative of the performance and strength of the process as a whole, especially as it relates to the effectiveness of the quality system and its success at delivering upon customer satisfaction and meeting customer expectations.

The Corporate Steering Team specifies statistical techniques for monitoring process and product and service characteristics, variables, and attributes. Department heads implement statistical techniques as specified and create appropriate reports and analyses. Department heads, the Corporate Steering Team, and others utilize

Prepared By	Ann Ova	Issue Number	3
Approved By	Damon Keith	Issue Date	7/2/93

ABC Typesetting Co.	Section 20.0	Page 2 of 2
Sample Quality Manual	STATISTICAL TECHNIQUES	

this information to make adjustments to the process and the quality system in order to better meet customer requirements and ensure customer satisfaction.

20.4 RELATED DOCUMENTATION

Details of the approved methods are contained in:

OP-20: Statistical Techniques

Prepared By	Ann Ova	Issue Number	3
Approved By	Damon Keith	Issue Date	7/2/93

Bibliography

American Society for Quality Control. *Quality Systems—Model for Quality Assurance in Design/Development, Production, Installation, and Servicing.* Milwaukee, WI, 1987.

American Society for Quality Control. *Quality Systems—Model for Quality Assurance in Final Inspection and Test.* Milwaukee, WI, 1987.

American Society for Quality Control. *Quality Systems—Model for Quality Assurance in Production and Installation.* Milwaukee, WI, 1987.

American Society for Quality Control. *Quality Management and Quality Assurance Standards—Guidelines for Selection and Use.* Milwaukee, WI, 1987.

American Society for Quality Control. *Quality Management and Quality System Elements—Guidelines.* Milwaukee, WI, 1987.

Barlas, Stephen. "U.S. Companies Feverishly Seek ISO 9000 Registration," *Managing Automation,* March 1992, p. 70.

Benson, Tracy E. "Quality Goes International," *Industry Week,* August 19, 1991, p. 55.

Berkman, Barbara N. "European Companies Join the Quality Crusade," *Electronic Business,* October 16, 1989, p. 263.

Costanzo, Anthony. "U.S. Corporate Executive Knowledge of ISO 9000 Lacking," *Quality,* September 1992, p. 47.

Graham, John F. "ISO-9000 Certification: Maintenance's Role," *Plant Services,* November 1991, p. 10.

Hutchens, Spencer. "Facing the ISO-9000 Challenge," *Compliance Engineering,* Fall 1991, p. 19.

International Organization for Standardization. *ISO 9000: International Standards for Quality Management,* 2d ed., Geneva, Switzerland, 1992.

Johnson, Gary. "American Firms Face Challenge of Meeting New Quality Guidelines," *Denver Business,* June/July 1991, p. 44.

Johnson, Perry L. *Keeping Score: Strategies and Tactics for Winning the Quality War.* New York: HarperBusiness, 1989.

Kiplinger Washington Letter, Vol. 69, No. 43, October 23, 1992.

Lamprecht, James L. *ISO 9000: Preparing for Registration.* New York: Marcel Dekker, Inc., 1992.

Niese, Ann. "ISO 9000: International Standard for Quality," *Electronic News,* November 1992.

Perry Johnson, Inc. *All About ISO 9000.* Text by Perry L. Johnson and Rob Kantner. Southfield, MI, 1992.

Perry Johnson, Inc. *How to Write Your ISO 9000 Quality Manual.* Text by Perry L. Johnson and Rob Kantner. Southfield, MI, 1992.

Placek, Chester. "Agreement on Standards, Testing, and Certification Outpacing Agreement on Many Other Issues Facing European Community," *Quality,* October 1991, p. 13.

Placek, Chester. "The ISO 9000 Edge," *Quality,* January 1992, p. 5.

Stratton, John H. "What Is the Registrar Accreditation Board?" *Quality Progress,* January 1992, p. 67.

Tiratto, Joseph. "Preparing for EC 1992 in the US Through Quality System Registration," *Computer,* April 1991.

Webb, Nanette M. "Flies in the Soup," *Quality in Manufacturing,* July/August 1991, p. 14.

Index

About the Author

Perry L. Johnson is founder and president of Perry Johnson, Inc., of Southfield, Michigan, a full-service consulting firm specializing in total quality management and ISO 9000 training and implementation. In the past decade, PJI has provided training to employees in more than 12,000 organizations throughout North America and Europe and implemented quality programs in more than 500 facilities. Its European affiliates have guided more than 200 facilities in ISO 9000 registration. The firm's products and services are listed in the U.S. government's GSA schedule; its ISO 9000 lead assessor training course is one of the few American courses to be registered by Britain's IQA/RBA. Mr. Johnson is also the author of *Keeping Score: Strategies and Tactics for Winning the Quality War.*